ALSO BY JOHN PAUL STEVENS

Five Chiefs

SIX
AMENDMENTS

*How and Why We Should
Change the Constitution*

—◇—

John Paul Stevens

LITTLE, BROWN AND COMPANY

LARGE PRINT EDITION

Little, Brown and Company
Hachette Book Group
237 Park Avenue, New York, NY 10017
littlebrown.com

First Edition: April 2014

Little, Brown and Company is a division of Hachette Book Group, Inc. The Little, Brown name and logo are trademarks of Hachette Book Group, Inc.

The publisher is not responsible for websites (or their content) that are not owned by the publisher.

The Hachette Speakers Bureau provides a wide range of authors for speaking events. To find out more, go to hachettespeakersbureau.com or call (866) 376-6591.

ISBN 978-0-316-33376-4

LCCN 2014933880

10   9   8   7   6   5   4   3   2   1

RRD-C

Printed in the United States of America

To my beautiful dietitian

Contents

————◦————

Prologue   3

Chapter I: The "Anti-Commandeering"
              Rule   19

Chapter II: Political Gerrymandering   43

Chapter III: Campaign Finance   77

Chapter IV: Sovereign Immunity   111

Chapter V: The Death Penalty   149

Chapter VI: The Second Amendment
              (Gun Control)   173

Appendix: Constitution of the United States   187

Acknowledgments   239

SIX
AMENDMENTS

Prologue

———◇———

According to its preamble, the Constitution of the United States was established by "the People" — not by the states — "in Order to form a more perfect Union, establish Justice, insure domestic Tranquility, provide for the common defence, promote the general Welfare, and secure the Blessings of Liberty to ourselves and our Posterity..." As Abraham Lincoln perceptively observed, it created a government "of the people, by the people, and for the people."

The Union created by the Constitution was unquestionably "more perfect" than the one formed by the states when they signed the Articles of Confederation. Under the Articles there was no central government authorized to resolve disputes among individual citizens, to tax or to impose any direct obligations on individuals, or to regulate commerce between or among the separate states. Like a treaty among multiple sovereigns, the Articles defined obligations that the former colonies assumed in their dealings with one another.

Despite the fact that the Constitution was far "more perfect" than its predecessor, important imperfections in its text were the product of compromises that were certain to require that changes be made in the future. Differing interests of large states and smaller states, as one example, and of slave states and free states, as another, required that the framers make significant concessions to secure agreement. Best known is the compromise that led to a bicameral legislature, with the Senate providing equal representation for all states and the House providing greater representation for the larger states. Less well known is the compromise that granted slave states two special benefits. Evidence of the importance of both of those compromises is found in Article V, which describes how the Constitution may be amended.

That article authorizes two methods of proposing new amendments—by two-thirds of both houses of Congress or by a convention for proposing amendments called by the legislatures of two-thirds of the states; and two methods of ratifying amendments—by the legislatures of three-fourths of the states, or by conventions in three-fourths of the states (this latter method has never been successfully used). Article V also prohibited two kinds of amendments. One of those prohibitions—the total ban on any amendment that would deprive any state, without its consent, "of its equal Suffrage in the Senate"—reveals that the framers viewed that body, rather than the executive or the judiciary, as the primary guardian of the sovereignty of the smaller states.

The second limitation on the power to amend the Constitution highlights the importance of the compromise that appeased the slave states. That limitation prohibited any amendment prior to 1808 that would allow Congress to regulate the importation of slaves. Article V did not, however, mention the bonus provided to the slave states in Article I's formula for granting them representation in Congress. Even though slaves were not allowed to vote in any state in the South, three-fifths of them were counted for the purpose of determining the size of a state's congressional delegation and the number of its votes in the Electoral College. In 1800 that slave bonus gave Thomas Jefferson more than the eight votes that provided his margin of victory over John Adams in the Electoral College. Not only did that bonus determine the outcome of that presidential election, but it also affected the work of Congress in the ensuing years when the interests of slave states and free states differed.

The procedures for amending the Constitution set forth in Article V have been successfully employed only eighteen times during the nation's history. On the first occasion, the ten amendments, often described as the Bill of Rights, were all adopted at once; they placed specific limits on the powers of the new central government. Thus, the First Amendment begins with the command that "Congress shall make no law respecting an establishment of religion," the preamble to the Second Amendment states that a "well regulated Militia [is] necessary to the security of a free State," and the Third Amendment protects homeowners from the quartering of soldiers in time of peace. The Fourth Amendment protects individuals from unreasonable searches and seizures. The Fifth Amendment, appropriately, includes five separate guarantees: (1) the right to indictment by a grand jury in felony or capital cases; (2) protection against self-incrimination or (3) double jeopardy; (4) the right not to be deprived of life, liberty, or property without due process of law; and (5) the right to just compensation when property is taken for public use. The Sixth Amendment protects the right to a prompt and public trial, the right to confront hostile witnesses, and the right to a lawyer. The Seventh Amendment protects the right to a jury trial in civil cases, and the Eighth Amendment prohibits excessive fines and cruel and unusual punishments. The Ninth Amendment provides that the enumeration of specific rights in the Constitution "shall not be construed to deny or disparage others retained by the people." And the Tenth Amendment provides that the "powers not delegated to the United States by the Constitution, nor prohibited by it to the States, are reserved to the States respectively, or to the people." It is undisputed that when they were adopted, the first ten amendments applied only to the federal government and placed no limits on the powers of the states.

Only two additional amendments were adopted prior to the Civil War. The Eleventh Amendment was a response to the Court's decision in February of 1793 to accept jurisdiction of an action against the state of Georgia brought by a citizen of South Carolina named Chisholm to recover the price of military supplies sold to the state during the Revolutionary War. The amendment precludes federal jurisdiction over cases against a state brought by citizens of another state. Some critics of the *Chisholm* decision, who believed that the common-law doctrine of sovereign immunity should have foreclosed the suit, have argued that the fact that the amendment was adopted so promptly proves that the Court's decision came as a "shock" to the nation, which believed that the framers had left intact the sovereign immunity of the states for these types of suits. In fact, however, the amendment that was ultimately adopted was not proposed until March 4, 1794, more than a year after the *Chisholm* case was decided, and more than eleven additional months elapsed before it was ratified. In contrast to that two-year deliberative process, the interval between the proposal on December 9, 1803, of the Twelfth Amendment — which significantly revised the Electoral College procedures used to elect the president — and its ratification on June 15, 1804, was just a few days more than six months.

President Abraham Lincoln played a major role in persuading Congress to propose the Thirteenth Amendment on January 31, 1865. That amendment, which abolished slavery, was not ratified by the states until December 6, well after his assassination on Good Friday in 1865.

The Fourteenth Amendment, which awarded citizenship to the former slaves, was opposed by President Andrew Johnson and not ratified until July 9, 1868. That amendment was immensely important, not only because it granted African Americans citizenship, but also because it imposed on the states a federal duty to govern impartially. It provided that no state may "deprive any person of life, liberty, or property, without due process of law; nor deny to any person within its jurisdiction the equal protection of the laws."

Ulysses S. Grant was president on February 3, 1870, when the Fifteenth Amendment, which granted the former slaves the right to vote, was ratified. By maintaining federal troops in the Southern states, Grant made it possible for the new class of voters to affect the results of a number of state elections. At the end of his second term, in 1877, however, presumably as a result of the compromise that settled the dispute over the outcome of the presidential election of 1876 by awarding the victory to Rutherford B. Hayes, the federal troops were withdrawn and white

supremacist groups like the Ku Klux Klan effectively put an end to African American voting in
the South for the next eighty years. During that
period, while the three-fifths slave bonus had
been eliminated by Section 2 of the Fourteenth
Amendment, the Southern states' congressional
delegations were enlarged by counting 100 percent of their African American populations,
even though the discriminatory administration
of local election laws combined with the terror-
ist tactics of the Klan prevented all but a few of
them from actually voting. Thus, one could
argue, the Southern states went from having a
three-fifths bonus before the Civil War to having a five-fifths bonus during this period.

In 1913 two amendments to the Constitution
were adopted. The Sixteenth Amendment overruled the five-to-four decision of the Supreme
Court in *Pollock* v. *Farmers Loan and Trust Co.*,[1]

---

1 158 U.S. 429 (1895). (This citation means that the opinion
may be found at page 429 of volume 158 of the United States Reports,
the official publication of the opinions of the United States Supreme
Court. The parenthetical at the end indicates that the opinion was
published in 1895.)

which had held that a federal statute imposing a tax on income violated the constitutional prohibition against unapportioned "direct taxes"; that amendment is the source of the federal power to impose an income tax. The Seventeenth Amendment replaced the practice of having United States senators chosen by state legislatures with direct elections by the people.

The Eighteenth Amendment, prohibiting the manufacture, sale, or transportation of intoxicating liquors, became effective in 1919; it was repealed by Section 1 of the Twenty-first Amendment in 1933. Section 2 of that amendment prohibited the transportation of intoxicating liquors into any state that prohibited their use. While nationwide prohibition was in effect, the Nineteenth Amendment gave women the right to vote, and the Twentieth Amendment advanced the commencement of the president's term in office from March 4 to January 20.

The Twenty-second Amendment, adopted in 1951, when Harry Truman was president, formally endorsed George Washington's decision that two terms as president were sufficient and rejected the possibility that a candidate as popular as Truman's predecessor, Franklin Delano Roosevelt (who had been elected four times), might be elected more than twice. The Twenty-third Amendment gave the District of Columbia representation in the Congress and in the Electoral College. The ratification of the Twenty-fourth Amendment in 1964 finally abolished the poll tax in federal elections. The Twenty-fifth Amendment, which became effective in 1967, specified for the first time the procedures to be followed to fill a vacancy in the office of vice president and to respond to the temporary or permanent incapacity of the president. Those procedures were followed by Richard Nixon when he nominated Gerald Ford to become vice president after Spiro Agnew resigned. That amendment also provided that Ford should become president when Nixon resigned. In 1971, the Twenty-sixth Amendment gave citizens who are eighteen years or older the right to vote in both federal and state elections.

In the past forty years only one amendment has been adopted: the Twenty-seventh, prohibiting Congress from changing its salary between elections. It was first submitted to the states in 1789 but was not ratified until two centuries later, in 1992. In those forty years, however, rules crafted by a slim majority of the members of the Supreme Court have had such a profound and unfortunate impact on our basic law that resort to the process of amendment is warranted. One of those rules has changed the character and increased the cost of campaigns for public office, a second has changed the composition of the Congress as well as that of many state legislatures, and two others have unwisely curtailed the powers of Congress. Moreover, the Court's death penalty jurisprudence, while improperly enhancing the risk of executing an innocent defendant, has simultaneously removed the principal justification for retaining that penalty. And the Court's interpretation of the Second Amendment has given federal judges, rather than the people's elected representatives, the final authority to define the permissible scope of civilian regulation of firearms.

In the following pages I propose six amendments to the Constitution; the first four would nullify judge-made rules, the fifth would expedite the demise of the death penalty, and the sixth would confine the coverage of the Second Amendment to the area intended by its authors. The importance of reexamining some of these rules is already the subject of widespread public debate, but others have not received either the attention or the criticism that is warranted. For that reason, I shall begin with a discussion of the "anti-commandeering rule," which prevents the federal government from utilizing critical state resources, thus impairing the federal government's ability to respond to problems with a national dimension, and explain why it would be prudent to eliminate the rule before a preventable catastrophe occurs. Chapter II argues that an amendment prohibiting political gerrymanders would make the House of Representatives and several state legislatures more representative and more democratic. In Chapter III, which discusses some of the predictable consequences of the controversial *Citizens United* decision, I suggest that the Court's most serious error may well have been attributable to a portion of the 1976 opinion in *Buckley* v. *Valeo*,[2] the case in which the Court extensively reviewed the constitutionality of the numerous statutory provisions regulating political campaigns that were enacted by Congress following Richard Nixon's reelection in 1974. Chapter IV explains how the Court's increasingly aggressive reliance on the doctrine of sovereign immunity, an ancient rule that has been expanded to protect states and their agents from liability even though they violate the law, has resulted in the wholesale invalidation of acts of Congress. In Chapter V, I shall explain why the death penalty should be banned throughout the country. And finally, in Chapter VI, I propose adding five words to the text of the Second Amendment to return it to the intent of its authors.

---

2 424 U.S. 1 (1976).

PROLOGUE

As time passes, I am confident that the soundness of each of my proposals will become more and more evident, and that ultimately each will be adopted. The purpose of this book is to expedite that process and to avoid future crises before they occur.

I

The "Anti-Commandeering" Rule

—◦—

The second paragraph of Article VI of the Constitution — the "Supremacy Clause" — provides: "This Constitution, and the laws of the United States which shall be made in pursuance thereof; and all Treaties made, or which shall be made, under the Authority of the United States, shall be the supreme Law of the Land; and the Judges in every State shall be bound thereby, any Thing in the Constitution or Laws of any State to the Contrary notwithstanding."

In a decision from which four justices dissented, the Court recognized that this clause permits Congress to enact laws that impose federal duties on state judges, but concluded that it does not allow the federal government to require any other state officials to enforce federal rules of law. The ruling in that case unnecessarily and unwisely curtails the power of Congress to make use of state officials in the enforcement or administration of federal law. It creates a serious risk that the federal response to national catastrophes or acts of terrorism will be inadequate; it also impairs the efficient administration of ordinary federal programs. The potentially harmful consequences of this "anti-commandeering" rule are clearly sufficient to justify an amendment to the Constitution repudiating it.

In the aftermath of the murder of twenty first graders and six adults at the Sandy Hook Elementary School in Newtown, Connecticut, on December 14, 2012, the *New York Times* published an article describing serious omissions in the database used by the federal government in making background checks of prospective gun purchasers:

The gaps exist because the system is voluntary; the Supreme Court ruled in 1997 that the federal government cannot force state officials to participate in the federal background check system. As a result, when a gun dealer asks the F.B.I. to check a buyer's history, the bureau sometimes allows the sale to proceed even though the purchaser should have been prohibited from acquiring a weapon, because its database is missing the relevant records. While the database flaws do not appear to have been a factor in the Newtown, Conn., school massacre, they have been linked to other attacks, including the Virginia Tech mass murder in 2007.

The 1997 case to which the article referred was the Court's five-to-four decision in *Printz* v. *United States*,[1] in which the Court announced what has come to be known as the anticommandeering rule—a rule that prohibits

---

1 521 U.S. 898 (1997).

Congress from requiring state officials to perform federal duties.

In the *Printz* case the Court considered the constitutionality of a provision in Congress's ultimate response to the attempted assassination of President Ronald Reagan in 1981. His assailant, John Hinckley, who almost succeeded in killing the president and who seriously wounded Jim Brady, the president's press secretary, was found not guilty by reason of insanity. After prolonged hearings and over seven years of debates, in 1993 Congress finally enacted the Brady Handgun Violence Protection Act as an amendment to the Gun Control Act of 1968. The 1968 act had established a detailed federal scheme governing the distribution of firearms. The amendments to that scheme were described in the legislative history as a response to an "epidemic of gun violence," noting that 15,377 Americans had been murdered with firearms in 1992.

The new statute, known as the Brady Act, required the attorney general to establish a national instant-background-check system to prevent felons and persons with mental problems from buying guns. The act authorized $200 million in federal grants to the states to compensate them for their assistance in developing the national system. Congress directed the attorney general to have the new system in place by November 30, 1998. In the interim, the amendment provided that a firearms dealer, before making a sale, must give notice to the local chief law enforcement officer ("CLEO"), who was then required to make a "reasonable effort" to determine whether the proposed sale would be lawful.

Congress obviously expected local law enforcement officers to welcome the opportunity to participate in the interim background-check program. A "friend of the court" brief filed in the Supreme Court on behalf of groups representing "hundreds of thousands" of police officers, including the Fraternal Order of Police and the National Association of Police Organizations, expressed unqualified support for the act and explained why the burden imposed on local officials was trivial, while the benefits of the background checks were significant. (Between

1994 and 1996 background checks had prevented approximately 6,600 firearms sales each month to potentially dangerous persons.) Nevertheless, Jay Printz, the CLEO for Ravalli County, Montana, and Richard Mack, the CLEO for Graham County, Arizona, filed two separate actions challenging the constitutionality of the interim provisions of the Brady Act. Printz and Mack were both represented by Stephen A. Halbrook, a well-respected Virginia lawyer and author who had written at length about the right to bear arms protected by the Second Amendment. Halbrook persuaded both district judges that a federal mandate requiring local sheriffs to perform background checks, even on a temporary basis, was prohibited by the Supreme Court's ruling in the then-recent decision in *New York* v. *United States.* In that case (over the dissent of Justices Byron White, Harry Blackmun, and myself) the Court had invalidated a federal statute that required states either to enact legislation providing for the disposal of radioactive waste within their borders or to take title to the waste.

The Court of Appeals for the Ninth Circuit reversed the district court decisions and upheld the constitutionality of the Brady Act. In its opinion the appellate court pointed out that the reasoning in the Supreme Court's opinion in *New York* applied to federal statutes commanding state legislatures to enact specific laws, but not to the Brady Act's direction to CLEOs. It wrote:

> Although we concede that there is language in *New York* that lends support to the view of Mack and Printz, that language must be interpreted in the context in which it was offered. *New York* was concerned with a federal intrusion on the States of a different kind and much greater magnitude than any involved in the Brady Act. The constitutional evil that *New York* addressed was one recognized by several of the cases already cited: the federal government was attempting to direct the States to enact their own legislation or regulations according to a federal formula.

After their loss in the Court of Appeals, Printz and Mack successfully sought review in the Supreme Court, arguing that the distinction between forced legislation and requiring other action by state officials was not valid. In a five-to-four decision, the Court agreed with that argument and ruled in their favor. That majority opinion is the source of what is now known as the anti-commandeering rule.

It was an unusual opinion because the Court failed to cite either of the two earlier opinions that—had they not been overruled—would have provided more support for its position than those it did cite. The two uncited cases were the 1861 opinion by Chief Justice Roger Taney in *Kentucky* v. *Dennison*,[2] and the 1976 opinion by then-Justice William H. Rehnquist in *National League of Cities* v. *Usery*.[3]

In the former case the state of Kentucky had requested the Court to issue an order compelling the governor of Ohio to comply with Ken-

---

2 65 U.S. (24 How.) 66 (1860).
3 426 U.S. 833 (1976).

tucky's attempt to extradite Willis Lago, who had been charged in Kentucky with assisting a slave to run away from his master. In his opinion for the Court refusing to order Ohio to comply with Kentucky's extradition request, Chief Justice Taney wrote:

> [W]e think it clear that the Federal government, under the Constitution, has no power to impose on a state officer, as such, any duty whatsoever, and compel him to perform it; for if it possessed this power, it might overload the officer with duties which would fill up all his time, and disable him from performing his obligations to the state, and might impose on him duties of a character incompatible with the rank and dignity to which he was elevated by the state (pp. 107–108).

While Taney's reasoning in that case would have provided direct support for the outcome in *Printz,* in a 1987 case involving a request by Puerto Rico to the governor of Iowa for the extradition of a fugitive who had been accused of murder in Puerto Rico, the Court reconsidered its holding in *Kentucky* v. *Dennison* and overruled the case. In his opinion for the Court in *Puerto Rico* v. *Branstad*,[4] Justice Thurgood Marshall wrote that:

> *Kentucky* v. *Dennison* rests upon a foundation with which time and the currents of constitutional change have dealt much less favorably. If it seemed clear to the Court in 1861, facing the looming shadow of a Civil War, that "the Federal Government, under the Constitution, has no power to impose on a State officer, as such, any duty whatever, and compel him to perform it," ... basic constitutional principles now point as clearly the other way.... It would be superfluous to restate all the occasions on which this Court has imposed upon state officials a duty to obey the requirements of the Constitution, or

---

4 483 U.S. 219 (1987).

compelled the performance of such duties; it may suffice to refer to *Brown* v. *Board of Education,* and *Cooper* v. *Aaron.* The fundamental premise of the holding in *Dennison*—"that the States and the Federal Government in all circumstances must be viewed as coequal sovereigns"— is not representative of the law today....

Kentucky v. *Dennison* is the product of another time. The conception of the relation between the States and the Federal Government there announced is fundamentally incompatible with more than a century of constitutional development. Yet this decision has stood while the world of which it was a part has passed away.[5]

Justice Rehnquist's opinion for a narrow majority in *National League of Cities* v. *Usery (the Secretary of Labor)*[6] would also have provided support for the anti-commandeering rule if the

---

5 *Id.* at 227–230.
6 426 U.S. 833 (1976).

case had not been overruled. In that case the Court invalidated an act of Congress that required the states to comply with the Fair Labor Standards Act, reasoning that the federal statute impermissibly impaired the states' ability to act as sovereigns. What that opinion described as an "undoubted attribute of sovereignty" was the states' power to determine the wages and hours of their employees. Because the Rehnquist majority viewed those determinations as "functions essential to separate and independent existence," it held that "Congress may not abrogate the States' otherwise plenary authority to make them."[7]

Less than a decade after the decision in *National League of Cities,* Justice Harry Blackmun had second thoughts about the case and decided that it should be overruled. In *Garcia* v. *San Antonio Metropolitan Transit Authority*[8] — a case that involved the application of the Fair Labor Standards Act to the employees of a pub-

---

7 *Id.* at 845–846.
8 469 U.S. 528 (1985).

lic agency—he did just that. Joined by the four justices who had dissented in *National League of Cities* (William J. Brennan, White, Marshall, and myself), he issued an opinion expressly overruling *National League of Cities*. In that opinion Justice Blackmun correctly explained that the states' sovereign interests "are more properly protected by procedural safeguards inherent in the structure of the federal system than by judicially created limitations on federal power."[9] Those procedural safeguards ensure that any decision to impose a federal duty on states or state officers, or the chief law enforcement officers of a county, is made by the Congress, all of whose members represent the interests of the several states.

Justice Blackmun's belief that the framers of the Constitution relied primarily on Congress rather than the judiciary to protect the states' sovereign interests is buttressed by the provision in Article V of the Constitution that permanently

---

9 *Garcia* v. *San Antonio Metropolitan Transit Authority,* 469 U.S. 528, 552 (1985).

prohibits any amendment that would deprive any state of its equal suffrage in the Senate. While he did not cite Article V in his *Garcia* opinion, his decision to defer to the congressional judgment expressed in the amendment to the Fair Labor Standards Act provides a dramatic contrast with the bold lawmaking approach followed by the majority in *Printz*.

That majority also failed to consider whether the rule it announced was really just "the product of another time," or whether deference was due to a decision made by the elected representatives of the states. Moreover, the opinion had little to say about the practical consequences of a decision limiting the power of the federal government to respond to problems with a national dimension. Instead, after stating that "there is no constitutional text speaking" to the question whether Congress can compel state officers to execute federal laws (a statement that simply ignores the text of the Supremacy Clause), the majority based its answer on (1) its understanding of relevant historical events, (2) what it described as "the structure of the Constitution," and (3) the Court's prior jurisprudence. While the debates between the majority and the four dissenters over those three matters occupy more than seventy pages in the official reports of the Court's decisions, a few words here will identify the nature of that debate.

The earliest historical events relevant to the *Printz* case were laws enacted by Congress in the 1790s; they required state judges to perform duties related to the registration of aliens, the naturalization of new citizens, and the arbitration of disputes about the seaworthiness of vessels. Under the majority's view those laws were authorized by the Supremacy Clause of the Constitution only because they imposed duties on state judges rather than on other state officers or agents. In my judgment that is not a fair reading of the text, which provides that "the Laws of the United States . . . shall be the supreme Law of the Land; and the Judges in every State shall be bound thereby" (Article VI, Cl. 2). Moreover, there were later historical events in which the federal government relied on state officials to carry out federal programs.

The World War I selective draft law was just such an event. The statute expressly authorized the president to utilize the services of "any or all departments and any or all agents of the United States and of the several States," and made it a misdemeanor for any person to refuse to comply with the president's directions. The statute provides an example of how reliance on state officials can provide an integral part of an important federal program. Whether it is also evidence of a belief shared by both the Congress and President Wilson that the federal government could *command* state participation — as opposed to merely making a *request* for voluntary assistance — was the subject of debate among the justices in the *Printz* case. The Court discounted the significance of this statute because, when President Wilson called upon the state governors to implement it, he "requested" them to act instead of issuing "commands." It seemed to me that the imposition of criminal sanctions for refusing to comply with a presidential request made it as mandatory as an express command. Moreover, it is unrealistic to assume that Congress would have enacted a national draft law—or that the president would have signed a law—that gave the separate states an option to refuse to participate, or to curtail their respective participation, in the nation's war effort. I think it also quite wrong to assume that a failure by Congress or the president to issue direct commands to state officers is evidence of a lack of power to do so. But even if we assume that the *Printz* majority correctly divined the actual intent of either President Wilson or the World War I Congress, that assumption sheds no light whatsoever on the wisdom of a rule that gives state and county officials a constitutional right to refuse to obey federal commands. The selective service law, which imposes a duty on ordinary citizens to engage in combat with our foreign enemies when ordered to do so, does, however, highlight the unusual character of a rule that gives county law enforcement officers a constitutional right to refuse to participate in a federal program designed to curb domestic violence.

The structure of the government created

under the Constitution differed from that created by the Articles of Confederation in several ways. Most relevant to the issue presented by *Printz,* under the Articles the national government had no direct power over individual citizens; its commands were all directed to the states, which in turn imposed duties on their citizenry. Under the Constitution both the states and the federal government exercise direct authority over citizens. The *Printz* majority made the illogical assumption that the Constitution's grant of additional authority to the national government must have been accompanied by a surrender of the preexisting authority to issue commands to states. It is more logical, however, to assume that an effective remedy for weakness would include not only the new authority but also the preservation of the existing authority. The fact that throughout our history the federal government has required the states to play a critical role in providing the manpower to fight our wars demonstrates that the anti-commandeering rule was invented by the *Printz* majority.

In addition to increasing the risk of a national catastrophe and hampering the federal government's ability to make a prompt and effective response to disasters, the anti-commandeering rule also limits the government's options in the routine administration of its programs. Federal programs involving the protection of the environment, the distribution of electric power, and the regulation of interstate transportation, as examples, may be implemented more efficiently by the reliance, in part, on state personnel instead of enlarging the federal bureaucracy. An article in the 1998 edition of the *Supreme Court Review* published by University of Chicago professors Matthew Adler and Seth Kreimer had this to say: "Like the federalism jurisprudence set forth a generation ago, in *National League of Cities* v. *Usery,* the new jurisprudence of commandeering purports to define an area of total state (and local) immunity from federal intervention. Neither the magnitude of the federal interest nor the degree of interference with state prerogatives is relevant. Rather, the doctrinal boundaries constitute what Justice Anthony

Kennedy calls 'the etiquette of federalism,' and federal trespass across those boundaries is per se invalid."

After noting that other scholars had already shown that neither history nor constitutional text supported the new doctrine, their own analysis "emboldened" Professors Adler and Kreimer to make "the positive prediction that the doctrine will soon be abandoned, as was *National League of Cities* a generation ago. A jurisprudence that consists of nothing more than some arbitrary rules of 'etiquette' ought to be, and we hope soon will be, outgrown."

Rather than waiting for a jurisprudence consisting of nothing more than an arbitrary rule of etiquette to be outgrown, I have come to the conclusion that the potential hazards associated with the rule are sufficiently serious to justify amending the Constitution to eliminate the rule. Even though each such hazard may be remote, the magnitude of the potentially harmful consequences is sufficiently serious to justify such action. Adding just four words—"and other public officials"—immediately after the word "Judges" in the Supremacy Clause would, under the Court's reasoning, expressly confirm the power of Congress to impose mandatory duties on public officials in every state.

I have already mentioned the fact that the voluntary character of state participation in the development of a database for making background checks of prospective gun purchasers enhances the risk that another mass murder will occur. Although the attack on the World Trade Center that occurred on September 11, 2001, was not foreseen when the *Printz* case was decided, I had this to say in my dissent:

> [S]ince the ultimate issue is one of power, we must consider its implications in times of national emergency. Matters such as the enlistment of air raid wardens, the administration of a military draft, the mass inoculation of children to forestall an epidemic, or perhaps the threat of an international terrorist, may require a

national response before federal personnel can be made available to respond.[10]

As Justice Breyer pointed out in his own dissent in the *Printz* case:

I would add to the reasons Justice Stevens sets forth the fact that the United States is not the only nation that seeks to reconcile the practical need for a central authority with the democratic virtues of more local control. At least some other countries, facing the same basic problem, have found that local control is better maintained through application of a principle that is the direct opposite of the principle the majority derives from the silence of our Constitution. The federal systems of Switzerland, Germany, and the European Union, for example, all provide that constituent states, not federal bureaucracies, will themselves implement many of

---

10 521 U.S. at 940.

the laws, rules, regulations, or decrees enacted by the central "federal" body.[11]

Perhaps Congress would seldom elect to pattern an American program after a foreign model, but our elected representatives, rather than judges, should decide whether it is wise to do so. They should take prompt action to minimize the risk of another tragedy like the massacre that occurred at the Sandy Hook Elementary School and to maximize the federal government's ability to respond effectively to natural disasters that recur with distressing frequency. The Constitution should be amended by adding the four words "and other public officials" to the Supremacy Clause in Article VI.

11 521 U.S., at 976.

II

Political Gerrymandering

What Justice Antonin Scalia described in an opinion written in 2004 as "severe partisan gerrymanders" are, in his judgment, incompatible with democratic principles. Neither he nor (as far as I am aware) any other federal judge has ever denied that such gerrymanders violate the Constitution. The extensive judicial debate that has persisted for years is whether it is for the courts to say when a violation has occurred and to design a remedy. During that debate, I do not believe any judge has had anything good to say about partisan gerrymanders. There should, therefore, be overwhelming support for an amendment to the Constitution that merely requires federal judges to apply the same rules in cases challenging political gerrymanders that they have applied to racial gerrymanders.

During the early history of Massachusetts the Federalists usually controlled the state government. In 1811, however, the governor, Elbridge Gerry, and a majority of both branches of the legislature were Republicans. In order to retain control of the government, on February 12, 1812, they redrew the boundaries of the thirty senatorial districts, packing enough Federalists into a small number of districts to give the Republicans comfortable majorities in the others. Of the 101,930 votes cast in the 1812 election, a majority of 51,766 were Federalist, but they elected only 11 senators. The Republican minority with only 50,164 votes elected 29 senators. The shapes of the districts drawn by Gerry's partisans were anything but compact. Because one of them resembled a salamander, contemporary newsmen coined the term "gerrymander" to describe the governor's electoral stratagem. Both the term and the stratagem have survived for the past two centuries.

Over the years the term has been used to describe two different varieties of election districts: racial gerrymanders and political gerrymanders. The Court has consistently condemned the former but has repeatedly floundered when confronted with the latter, even though the same standards could easily have been applied to both.

In 1960, in *Gomillion* v. *Lightfoot*,[1] the Court unanimously held that the Alabama legislature could not change the boundaries of the City of Tuskegee "from a square to an uncouth twenty-eight-sided figure" in order to deprive all but a few of the African Americans residing within the square of their right to vote in city elections. The Court's opinion, written by Justice Felix Frankfurter, held that the gerrymander violated the Fifteenth Amendment, which protects the right to vote from discrimination "on account of race, color, or previous condition of servitude." Justice Charles Whittaker thought

1 364 U.S. 339 (1960).

the change in the city's boundaries violated the Fourteenth rather than the Fifteenth Amendment, but otherwise agreed with the Court's conclusion. Under either theory, the shape of the district, together with its effect on blacks, provided a sufficient basis for concluding that it was invalid.

Three decades later, the Court considered the constitutionality of redistricting motivated by racial considerations quite unlike those at play in *Gomillion*. In 1991, in an attempt to comply with the federal Voting Rights Act of 1965, North Carolina enacted a congressional districting plan that included a majority-black district resembling a snake that was 160 miles long. This triggered litigation that led to two important decisions; one in 1993 addressing North Carolina's plan and a second in 1995 dealing with Georgia's congressional redistricting. In both of these cases, decided by five-to-four majorities, the Court invalidated the challenged plans because it concluded that the dramatically irregular shapes of the new districts constituted unconstitutional gerrymanders. The four dissenters thought that race-conscious redistricting for the purpose of benefiting minority voters was permissible, but the Court disagreed. While it recognized that a state legislature is not entirely prohibited from acting with consciousness of race, it concluded that racial gerrymandering is impermissible whenever race was the legislature's "dominant and controlling rationale" in drawing its district lines. There is no reason why that test should not also apply to political gerrymanders like the one that Governor Gerry and his fellow Republicans designed in 1812.

While a state legislature is not entirely prohibited from acting with a consciousness of politics, naked partisan advantage should not provide the "dominant and controlling rationale" in drawing district lines. Three characteristics identify every political gerrymander. First, it is the product of decisions made by a political party in control of a state government; second, it benefits that party by increasing the number of elections that its candidates will win; and third, it contains districts that are anything but compact—districts with bizarre shapes that prompt observers to question the motives of their architects. Maps of districts designed by New Jersey Democrats in 1982 (Exhibit 1 in the insert), by Texas Democrats in 1991 (Exhibit 2 in the insert), and by Pennsylvania Republicans in 2002 (Exhibit 3 in the insert) illustrate this third point.

The effects of gerrymanders are well known and well documented. Not only do they enable political majorities to prolong their control of state governments, but they also distort some states' representation in the Congress of the United States. A recent *New York Times* story noted that in Illinois, where Democrats drew the maps, Republican candidates for Congress won 45 percent of the popular vote but only a third of the House seats, and in Maryland, where Democrats also drew the maps, Republicans won 35 percent of the votes but only 13 percent of the congressional seats. On the other hand, in states where Republicans were in control, their candidates for Congress won 71 percent of the seats with only about 56 percent of the vote. In states where courts or independent commissions drew the maps, the percent of the popular vote roughly matched the percent of electoral victories for both parties. In addition, the gerrymandering process makes elections—both in districts the majority expects to carry and in districts packed with voters who belong to the minority party—less competitive. For candidates who have no fear of losing to a member of the opposite party, the primary rather than the general election will be the decisive event in their campaigns. Whether liberal or conservative, candidates can be expected to adopt more extreme positions when competing within a single party than when competing with a member of the opposite party. I firmly believe that gerrymandering has made our elected officials more doctrinaire and less willing to compromise with members of the opposite party. It may well have been the principal cause of the government shutdown that occurred in October 2013.

Congress has addressed the problem of gerrymandering spasmodically and ineffectively. The Apportionment Act of 1842 provided that representatives must be elected from single-member districts that are composed of contiguous territory. In 1872 Congress added a requirement that the districts contain "as nearly as possible" an equal number of inhabitants. Apportionment legislation enacted in 1901 and 1911 included a further requirement that districts be compact. In neither of those statutes did Congress define the term "compact," presumably because it assumed that the meaning of the word was well understood by the ordinary reader. As the following excerpt from *Webster's Third New International Dictionary* indicates, it is a term that is most easily understood by describing shapes that are not compact. For *Webster's*, a compact district is "located within a limited definite space without straggling or rambling over a wide area." The contiguity and compactness requirements were omitted from later federal redistricting requirements. Several states have, however, enacted their own laws that either regulate the shapes of districts or prescribe procedures that insulate the redistricting process from partisan politics.

Over the years the Supreme Court jurisprudence dealing with political gerrymanders can best be described as wishy-washy. Prior to its decision in *Gomillion* v. *Lightfoot* in 1960, the Court scrupulously avoided what Justice Frankfurter described as the "political thicket." For example, in 1946 it refused to review the constitutionality of an Illinois statute enacted in 1901 that gave equal representation to districts that varied in size from 112,000 to 900,000. Under that statute an individual vote in the smallest district had almost nine times the value of a vote in the most populated district. In 1962, however, over Justice Frankfurter's dissent, the Court decided *Baker* v. *Carr*,[2] in which it upheld a voter's right to challenge a Tennessee statute similar to the Illinois statute as violating the Fourteenth Amendment's Equal Protection Clause. Then, in 1964, as a sequel to *Baker* v. *Carr*'s entry into the political thicket, Chief Justice Earl Warren's opinion in *Reynolds* v. *Sims*[3] announced the "one person, one vote" rule requiring that districts contain equal numbers

---

2 369 U.S. 186 (1962).
3 377 U.S. 533 (1964).

of voters. In announcing that new rule, both the chief justice writing for the majority and Justice John Harlan in his dissent recognized that an exclusive focus on the size of districts would often require abandonment of natural or historic boundary lines, and therefore provide "an open invitation to partisan gerrymandering."

As noted above, Exhibit 1 provides persuasive evidence that the Democrats in control of New Jersey's government in 1982 accepted that invitation.

Before New Jersey did so, in a case involving a Missouri districting plan, the Court decided that the rule requiring equal representation for equal numbers of people required the states to make a good faith effort to achieve precise mathematical equality after every decennial census: "Unless population variances among districts are shown to have resulted despite such effort, the State must justify each variance, no matter how small."[4] In his opinion for the Court, Justice Brennan then rejected each justification

---

4 *Kirkpatrick* v. *Preisler*, 394 U.S. 526, 530 (1969).

offered by Missouri—including its claim that some of the deviations from equality were justified by an attempt to ensure that each congressional district would be geographically compact. He concluded the Court's opinion with this sentence: "A State's preference for pleasingly shaped districts can hardly justify population variances."[5]

In separate opinions, Justices Abe Fortas, Harlan, Potter Stewart, and White disagreed with the strict standard announced by the Court. They would have found minor deviations from strict numerical equality acceptable. Justice Fortas nevertheless concurred in the Court's judgment because there was "no finding of gerrymandering."[6] Writing in dissent for himself and Justice Stewart, Justice Harlan argued that the Court's "rule of absolute equality is perfectly compatible with 'gerrymandering' of the worst sort."[7] In his dissent, Byron White quoted the passage from Chief Justice Warren's opinion

---

5 *Id.* at 536.
6 *Id.* at 541.
7 *Id.* at 551.

in *Reynolds* v. *Sims,* noting that "[i]ndiscriminate districting, without any regard for political subdivision or natural or historical boundary lines, may be little more than an open invitation to partisan gerrymandering."[8]

The debate between the majority led by Justice Brennan, favoring precise numerical equality, and Justice White, who would have tolerated minor numerical differences among districts, was renewed in 1983 after I joined the Court. The case, *Karcher* v. *Daggett,*[9] involved a challenge by Republicans to a New Jersey districting plan that included 527,472 people in the largest district and 523,798 in the smallest; thus each had a population that differed from the average by less than 1 percent. The plan had been adopted by a state legislature controlled by Democrats and signed by the outgoing Democratic governor Brendan Byrne only hours before Tom Kean, the newly elected Republican governor, took office.

---

8 *Id.* at 553.
9 462 U.S. 725 (1983).

The Democrats had been in control of the state government during the four-year period that began on January 20, 1978. The boost to the strength of the Republican Party that accompanied Ronald Reagan's election to the presidency in 1980 made it likely, though of course not certain, that there would be a change in the control of the state government in 1982. That change did occur on January 20, 1982, after the closest gubernatorial election in New Jersey's history. Prior to Kean's inauguration, as a result of the 1980 census the size of New Jersey's congressional delegation, which had included eight Democrats and seven Republicans, was reduced from fifteen to fourteen, making it necessary to redraw the district boundaries. In the first election under the new plan drawn by the outgoing Democrats, their party won nine seats and the Republicans won only five, despite Reagan's continuing popularity. (In the presidential election, two years earlier, he had beaten Carter by over 12 percent of the vote in New Jersey.)

The plan adopted by the Democratic majority

of the state legislature on the eve of the transfer of state power was challenged by Republicans who argued, first, that a different plan that they had supported would have come even closer to precise numerical equality, and, second, that the plan enacted into law had not been adopted in good faith. (Exactly what they meant by the term "good faith" is not at all clear; I assumed that they were contending that it violated the controlling party's duty to govern impartially.) The district court agreed with the plaintiffs' first submission. Even though the populations of the districts differed from one another by less than 1 percent, the fact that an alternate proposed by the Republicans had even smaller differences established a violation of the strict rule applied in the *Kirkpatrick* case.

On appeal to the Supreme Court, Justice Brennan wrote an opinion holding that the district court had properly applied the rule announced in *Kirkpatrick;* Justice White, joined by Chief Justice Warren Burger and Justices Lewis Powell and William Rehnquist, dissented, again arguing that the strict rule was unwise and should not be applied to a plan whose districts were as close to absolute equality as those in the New Jersey plan.

While I agreed with Justice White's criticism of the majority's strict rule, it seemed to me that the district court had correctly applied the law and that the difference between his approach and Brennan's was not sufficiently important to justify overruling the earlier decision in the *Kirkpatrick* case. I therefore joined the Brennan opinion, but in my own concurrence argued that the district court should have relied on the plaintiff's alternate contention that the grotesque shapes of the districts demonstrated that the plan had not been adopted in good faith. Unless the defendants could identify a neutral justification for the bizarre configuration of the districts, I said, they would qualify as political gerrymanders whose architects had violated their duty to govern impartially.

Because the shapes of the districts played such an important role in my argument, I instructed the Court's printer to include the map that appears as Exhibit 1 in this chapter in the official report of the case. Because the printer's budget did not contemplate spending about $3,000 to cover the cost of such a colored insert, it became necessary either to persuade Chief Justice Warren Burger that the expense was appropriate or to ask the full Court to overrule his budgetary decision. My proposed appeal to the full Court became unnecessary when the chief justice acknowledged that my chambers were responsible for saving the Court even more money than the cost of an occasional multicolored map, because I employed fewer law clerks than any of our colleagues. (For anyone eager to behold the color version of the map, it is located in the insert.)

I was, however, less successful in my attempt to convince any of them that New Jersey's new electoral districts should be invalidated as impermissible political gerrymanders. Lewis Powell did write a separate opinion endorsing my arguments but he did not join my opinion, because the district court had not relied on the petitioners' good faith argument. Presumably for that reason both Justice Brennan and Justice White simply ignored what I had to say.

Although the increase in partisan gerrymandering that followed the announcement and refinement of the "one person, one vote" rule did not come as a surprise, neither the Court nor any of its members has ever suggested that it was a desirable development.

Instead, the debate that did develop involved two different questions: do federal courts have jurisdiction to decide whether an alleged political gerrymander violates the Constitution; and, if so, what standard should govern the decision of such a case? Both of those questions were presented in the case of *Davis* v. *Bandemer*[10] decided in 1986.

In that case, two groups of plaintiffs challenged the statewide redistricting plan enacted by the Indiana legislature in 1981. Leaders of the Democratic Party claimed that it discriminated against the members of their party; the National Association for the Advancement of Colored People claimed that it discriminated against their members because of their race. The

---

10   478 U.S. 109 (1986).

three-judge district court rejected the latter claim because the evidence established that the plan's impact on black voters was merely a by-product of the intended adverse impact on Democrats rather than the result of racial animus. Relying on the reasoning in my separate opinion in *Karcher* v. *Daggett,* however, the majority of the district court did find that the Republicans in the Indiana legislature had specifically intended to make it more difficult for Democrats to win elections, that there was no other justification for the shape of the non-compact districts in the plan, and that the effect of the plan was to enable Republicans to win a significantly disproportionate share of the elections. As an example, while Republican candidates for seats in the statehouse received only 48.1 percent of the vote, they won 57 of the available 100 seats.

On their direct appeal to the United States Supreme Court, the Indiana Republicans argued both (1) that the gerrymandering claims were not "justiciable" because they raised the kinds of political questions that federal judges have no business deciding, and (2) on the merits, that the plaintiffs had failed to prove invidious discrimination. Justice White, joined by five other justices (Brennan, Marshall, Blackmun, Powell, and myself) rejected the first argument, but, joined by only the first three of those justices, accepted the second. (The justices who had dissented on the first issue—Burger, Rehnquist, and Sandra Day O'Connor—also agreed with White's conclusion on the second issue.)

The holding that the claims were justiciable rested on the premise that "each political group in a State should have the same chance to elect representatives of its choice as any other political group."[11] As Justice White explained, the fact that a "claim is submitted by a political group rather than a racial group does not distinguish it in terms of justiciability. That the characteristics of the complaining group are not immutable or that the group has not been subject to the same historical stigma may be relevant to the manner

---

11 478 U.S. at 124.

in which the case is adjudicated, but these differences do not justify a refusal to entertain such a case."[12] (Indeed, earlier opinions had authorized challenges to multimember districts that would "operate to minimize or cancel out the voting strength of racial *or political* elements of the voting population."[13]) Thus, for purposes of justiciability under the Equal Protection Clause of the Fourteenth Amendment, the same standard applied to discrimination against political groups as to that applied against racial groups.

In his discussion of the merits, however, Justice White misinterpreted the district court's decision and announced a brand-new requirement for establishing unconstitutional discrimination against a political group. Whereas the district court had correctly found that the evidence of election results producing a disproportionate number of victories for the Republicans was sufficient to prove an adverse impact on the plaintiffs, Justice White treated the decision as

---

12 *Id.* at 125.
13 *Id.* at 119.

having held that "any apportionment scheme that purposely prevents proportional representation is unconstitutional."[14] The novel requirement that Justice White announced in his opinion is a showing that the disadvantaged group "has been unconstitutionally denied its chance to effectively influence the political process."[15] Justice White further stated that any "such a finding of unconstitutionality must be supported by evidence of continued frustration of the will of a majority of the voters or effective denial to a minority of the voters of a fair chance to influence the political process."[16] Although the exact meaning of the new requirement is not entirely clear, it apparently assumes that the harm to the minority must entail more than the loss of an election because even losing elections may not entirely deprive the loser of the opportunity to influence the political process.

Admittedly, the Constitution does not require proportional representation, but there is a world

14 *Id.* at 129–130.
15 *Id.* at 132–133.
16 *Id.* at 133.

of difference between such a strict requirement and a more limited prohibition against a political party's use of governmental power to draft bizarre districts that have no purpose or justification other than enhancing that party's own power. Just as a controlling political party may not use public funds to pay its campaign expenses, it is also quite wrong to use public power for the sole purpose of enhancing the political strength of the majority party.

While I am sure that Justice White did not actually intend to create an impenetrable bar to recovery in cases challenging political gerrymanders, in the ensuing years his new requirement has never been satisfied. In my judgment the most realistic explanation for Justice White's opinion on the merits is a combination of a fear that an affirmance in the *Bandemer* case itself would have spawned a flood of federal litigation and an assumption that gerrymandering was a traditional form of cyclical political behavior that was really not all that serious.

His fear of an endless avalanche of litigation would be justified if every intended election result that departed from strict proportional representation were treated as an unconstitutional gerrymander. But all of the Court's racial gerrymandering cases involved districts with such grotesque shapes that there was little need for, or use of, additional evidence to prove the dominant motive of their draftsmen. Applying the same rule to political gerrymanders might generate an immediate increase in the volume of litigation, but such an increase would surely be temporary.

The volume of litigation that developed in the wake of the Court's "one person, one vote" ruling was substantial, but it diminished as states increasingly adhered to the new rule. Contemporary criticism of the Warren Court's "activism" and disregard for "states' rights" has been replaced by a general consensus that the rule was sound and serves the public interest. Litigation involving debates over the adequacy of state compliance with the rule still occurs, but I am not aware of any serious contention that the litigation costs outweigh the fairness interests that the rule serves.

A similar pattern of gerrymandering litigation might well have developed if the district court's judgment in *Bandemer* had been affirmed. It is nevertheless important to recognize that the case demonstrated that a trial court is fully capable of evaluating evidence proving the single-minded political purpose that motivated the crafting of noncompact districts. Affirmance would no doubt have generated more litigation, but strict enforcement of the district court's approach would, in time, have led to compliance with the law and the demise of a practice that has been viewed with disfavor throughout our history.

With respect to the notion that gerrymandering is simply an inevitable feature of partisan politics in America, I am reminded of my first exposure to the patronage system. "To the victor belongs the spoils" describes Andrew Jackson's appraisal of the benefits of winning an election in a democracy. Relying on that approach to partisan politics, in 1971 the newly elected Republican secretary of state of Illinois discharged 1,946 employees. Over 90 of them brought suit claiming that they had been fired because they refused to join the Republican Party and that a discharge of non-policy-making employees such as janitors and elevator operators for that reason was unconstitutional. The federal district judge dismissed their action because they had no contractual right to retain their jobs. The employees' dismissal was supported by Justice Holmes's famous dictum that a policeman "may have a constitutional right to talk politics, but he has no constitutional right to be a policeman." When I first looked at the case as a judge on the Court of Appeals for the Seventh Circuit, I had a similar reaction—when they were hired, the plaintiffs had presumably benefited from the same established political practice that they were now challenging. As two other appellate courts had recently held, "He who lives by the political sword must be prepared to die by the political sword." But after studying the briefs, it dawned on me that the case raised a more basic question. Does the acquisition of political power, whether by winning a partisan election or by receiving an appointment from a successful candidate, include the right to use that power for purely partisan purposes? It is similar to the question whether a political party may use public funds to pay campaign or personal expenses. Does the Constitution permit a Democratic chief of police to dismiss or refuse to hire police officers because they àre Republicans?

In the rather long opinion that I wrote in 1972 for that case, *Illinois State Employees Union* v. *Lewis,* I relied on the First Amendment to the Constitution in explaining my answer to that basic question: "While the patronage system is defended in the name of democratic tradition, its paternalistic impact on the political process is actually at war with the deeper traditions of democracy embodied in the First Amendment."[17] Four years later the Supreme Court

---

17 473 F. 2d 561, 576 (CA7, 1972), 473 F. 2d 561, 576 (CA7, 1972). (This citation is similar to the one used for the U.S. Reports. It indicates that the quotation may be found at page 576 of an opinion beginning on page 561 of volume 473 of the Federal Reporter, Second Series. The Federal Reporter, Second Series, contains decisions of the Courts of Appeals between 1924 and 1993. "CA7" tells the reader that the case was decided by the Seventh Circuit Court of Appeals.

endorsed my answer in a case challenging the patronage practices of the sheriff of Cook County. In his opinion Justice Brennan elaborated:

> [W]e are not persuaded that the elimination of patronage practice, or as is specifically involved here, the interdiction of patronage dismissals, will bring about the demise of party politics. Political parties existed in the absence of active patronage practice prior to the administration of Andrew Jackson, and they have survived substantial reduction in their patronage power through the establishment of merit systems.[18]

The Court followed that precedent in a 1980 case holding that the political affiliation of two public defenders was an impermissible basis for their discharge. In 1990 it went a step further when it held that applicants for public

The parenthetical at the end indicates that the opinion was published in 1972.)

18 *Elrod* v. *Burns,* 427 U.S. 347, 369 (1976).

employment cannot be rejected on the basis of their political affiliation. Finally, in a pair of opinions authored by Justice O'Connor and Justice Kennedy in 1996, the Court limited the patronage system even further in two cases involving independent government contractors. Justice Scalia, who was not on the Court when *Davis* v. *Bandemer* was decided but is now the Court's strongest supporter of the view that federal judges should never review political gerrymandering claims, had this to say in his dissent in those two cases: "[W]hen a practice not expressly prohibited by the text of the Bill of Rights bears the endorsement of a long tradition of open, widespread, and unchallenged use that dates back to the beginning of the Republic, we have no proper basis for striking it down."[19]

That is certainly not my view of how we should interpret the Constitution. After all, in its preamble the framers explained their purpose to form a "more perfect" Union, and over the

---

19 *Board of Comm'rs, Wabaunsee Cty.* v. *Umbehr,* 518 U.S. 668, 687 (1996).

years we have rejected more than one practice that had been open, widespread, and unchallenged for generations—segregated schools is perhaps the most obvious example. Patronage abuses and gerrymandering should be evaluated on their merits, not simply accepted because they have been in use for such a long time. A legal rule should not persist merely because of its unmerited longevity. That gerrymandering has a long history does not counsel in its favor.

Instead, gerrymandering should receive the same treatment as patronage. The public interest, rather than mere partisan advantage, should provide the basic standard that should govern the design of electoral districts as well as the employment of government personnel. As long as state legislatures set the boundaries of electoral districts, political and racial considerations will no doubt have some impact on the process. But there is no reason why partisans should be permitted to draw lines that have no justification other than enhancing their own power. Bizarre lines like those set forth in the record in *Davis* v. *Bandemer,* in the Texas redistricting case of *Bush* v. *Vera* (Exhibit 2), and in Exhibits 1 and 3 provide sufficient evidence of an improper purpose to impose a burden of explanation on the state. If a departure from compactness cannot be explained by reference to a neutral factor, such as a river, a highway, a boundary such as a county line, or changes in the district's population, the district should be redrawn.

Putting an end to gerrymandering will not only make state governments more representative, but also will have a beneficial impact on the composition of the House of Representatives for two reasons. The most obvious is the fact that the composition of state delegations will tend to reflect the political composition of the states instead of containing a surplus of members of the party that controls the districting process. But a second reason may be even more significant. As discussed above, the gerrymandering process makes elections—both in districts the majority expects to carry, and in districts packed with voters who belong to the minority party—less competitive, and leads candidates, whether liberal or conservative, to adopt more extreme positions. Ending political gerrymandering will help promote political compromise.

Adoption of the amendment that I propose would not only require that relief be awarded in a challenge to a statewide gerrymander like that condemned by the district court (and by Justice Powell and me in his dissent) in *Davis* v. *Bandemer,* but would also authorize relief in challenges to individual districts with bizarre shapes motivated entirely by partisan concerns. Exhibit 2 portrays the Pennsylvania district that was the subject of debate in the Supreme Court in 2004 in *Vieth* v. *Jubelirer.*[20] It is obvious that the district was not compact; the plaintiff, a Democrat, had offered to prove that partisan concerns had provided the sole motivation for its noncompact design, and that it had in fact produced a victory for the Republicans in the 2002 election. While the majority held that the Court should refuse to adjudicate the merits of the claim, no justice disagreed with the proposition that such

---

20 541 U.S. 267 (2004).

a gerrymander is incompatible with democratic principles and violates the Constitution. After all, the concept of equal justice under law, so fundamental to our jurisprudence that it is inscribed above the entrance to the Supreme Court, requires the states to govern impartially. As I explained in my dissent in *Vieth,* this means that "if no neutral criterion can be identified to justify the lines drawn, and if the only possible explanation for a district's bizarre shape is a naked desire to increase partisan strength," then such a district is a violation of a state's duty to govern impartially and an impermissible political gerrymander.[21] As our racial gerrymander cases demonstrate, the courts are fully capable of recognizing and remedying such a violation.

They would be required to do so if the following amendment were adopted:

Districts represented by members of Congress, or by members of any state legislative body, shall be compact and com-

---

21 *Id.* at 339.

posed of contiguous territory. The state shall have the burden of justifying any departures from this requirement by reference to neutral criteria such as natural, political, or historic boundaries or demographic changes. The interest in enhancing or preserving the political power of the party in control of the state government is not such a neutral criterion.

In part because I am persuaded that political gerrymandering played a major role in the events that led to the shutdown of the federal government in October 2013, I am also convinced that such an amendment should be promptly proposed and ratified.

III

Campaign Finance

———◆◇◆———

Federal statutes regulating the financing of political campaigns have drawn a basic distinction between two categories of speech — so-called campaign speech, which expressly advocates the election or defeat of specific candidates, and speech about general issues such as taxation, disaster relief, global warming, abortion, or gun control.

The law allows business corporations to form and operate political action committees (PACs) that are financed by voluntary contributions from their stockholders and employees. Expenditures by PACs are essentially unregulated because — unlike expenditures of a corporation's general funds — they do not impose a significant risk of using minority shareholders' money to support causes that those shareholders oppose.

Citizens United is a wealthy nonprofit corporation that runs a PAC with millions of dollars in assets. It is supported almost entirely by contributions from individuals, but it has received some funds from corporate donors. In 2008 it released a ninety-minute film about then-Senator Hillary Clinton, who was a potential candidate for president; the film's unambiguous opposition to her candidacy qualified it as campaign speech.

The Bipartisan Campaign Reform Act of 2002 (BCRA) prohibited corporations and unions from using general treasury funds to finance campaign speech during a period of thirty days before a primary election. In an opinion written jointly by Justice Sandra Day O'Connor and me in early 2003, the Court held that that prohibition was constitutional. Fearing that television advertisements about the movie, as well as the movie itself, might violate that prohibition, Citizens United brought suit against the Federal Election Commission seeking an injunction against enforcement of that statute, arguing that the movie was not an "electioneering communication" within the meaning of the statute and that the statute should not apply to a not-for-profit corporation. The district court denied relief and Citizens United appealed to the Supreme Court (campaign finance is regulated in a relatively unusual statutory scheme: a three-judge district court ruling is appealable directly to the Supreme Court). After hearing the initial argument, the Court ordered the parties to reargue the case and address the issue that had been recently decided in the opinion that Justice O'Connor and I had written in 2003. By a vote of five to four, the Court ruled for Citizens United and essentially held that corporations have an unlimited constitutional right to finance campaign speech.

I shall not repeat the arguments that I

advanced in my eighty-six-page dissent that Justices Ruth Bader Ginsburg, Stephen Breyer, and Sonia Sotomayor joined (and that Justice David Souter has told me he would have joined had he still been a member of the Court when the case was reargued). Instead, I shall explain why it is unwise to allow persons who are not qualified to vote—whether they be corporations or nonresident individuals—to have a potentially greater power to affect the outcome of elections than eligible voters have.

In his 1905 annual message to Congress, President Theodore Roosevelt declared,

> All contributions by corporations to any political committee for any political purpose should be forbidden by law; directors should not be permitted to use stockholders' money for such purposes; and, moreover, a prohibition of this kind would be, as far as it went, an effective method of stopping the evils aimed at in corrupt practices acts.

Two years later Congress passed a statute banning all corporate contributions to political candidates. For decades thereafter, Congress, most state legislators, and members of the Supreme Court apparently assumed that it was both wise and constitutional to impose greater restrictions on corporate participation in elections than on individuals.

As an example, in 1982 Justice William H. Rehnquist, writing for a unanimous Court in *Federal Election Commission* v. *National Right to Work Committee,* a case holding that Congress could prohibit not-for-profit corporations from soliciting funds from nonmembers for political purposes, stated that there is no reason why Congress's interest in preventing both actual corruption and the appearance of corruption of elected representatives may not "be accomplished by treating...corporations differently from individuals."[1] Such was the consensus that the first opinions written by any member of the Court arguing that corporate expenditures

---

1 459 U.S. 197, 210–211 (1982).

in election campaigns are entitled to the same constitutional protection as the activity of individual voters were not announced until 1990. Yet the dissenting opinions written by Justices Antonin Scalia and Anthony Kennedy in that year in *Austin* v. *Michigan Chamber of Commerce*[2] are unquestionably among the most significant writings on the subject of campaign financing by any justice. In those opinions, Justices Scalia and Kennedy advanced the arguments that later persuaded three of their future colleagues to join the majority in *Citizens United* v. *Federal Election Commission.*[3]

In the *Michigan Chamber of Commerce* case the Court had upheld the constitutionality of a Michigan statute that prohibited corporations from making any expenditure in connection with an election campaign for state office. The law made it a crime for the Chamber to pay for a newspaper advertisement announcing its support for a candidate seeking election to the

---

2 494 U.S. 652, 679, 695 (1990).
3 558 U.S. 310 (2010).

Michigan legislature. Justice Scalia dissented and argued that corporate speech, like other expressive activities by groups of persons, was entitled to the same First Amendment protection as speech by an individual. Justice Kennedy also dissented and contended that a speaker's identity as a corporation was an impermissible basis for regulating its speech or its expenditures financing speech. Two decades later, those same arguments provided the basis for the Court's five-to-four decision in *Citizens United* overruling the *Michigan Chamber of Commerce* case and apparently affording the same constitutional protection to election-related expenditures by corporations as to speech by individual voters.

———

Contributions to the campaign to reelect President Richard Nixon in 1972 were managed by the organization known by the acronym CRP (mocked as CREEP) — the Committee for the Re-Election of the President. Not all of those funds were used to finance expressive activities.

Some of them were in the possession of the five burglars who broke into the headquarters of the Democratic National Committee in the Watergate complex in Washington, D.C., on June 17, 1972, apparently for the purpose of obtaining information about the Democrats' campaign strategy. The break-in had a multitude of unintended and unexpected consequences. Especially important was the Supreme Court decision resolving a controversy between the special prosecutor and President Nixon that required him to surrender tape recordings of his private conversations. That decision shed a brilliant light on the power and independence of the federal judiciary; it led to the resignation of President Nixon and, in turn, to the succession of Gerald Ford to the presidency.[4] It is not, however, that consequence of Watergate that I shall discuss in this chapter. Instead, I shall identify a constitutional issue arising out of leg-

---

4 I suppose, therefore, that I can look back to the break-in as one of the "but-for" causes of President Ford's nomination of me to fill the vacancy produced by William O. Douglas's resignation from the Court.

islation enacted by Congress in response to the Watergate break-in; namely, whether limits on campaign expenditures may be justified by the interest in providing opposing candidates with an equal opportunity to persuade their fellow citizens to vote for them.

The legislation that followed the Watergate break-in applied new rules to a host of campaign-related issues that had nothing to do with the break-in itself. Among them were provisions limiting the amounts of money that could be contributed to candidates for federal office, as well as the amounts that candidates and their supporters could spend during their campaigns. The constitutionality of those limitations, as well as a number of other provisions of the Federal Election Campaign Act Amendments of 1974, was being reviewed by the Supreme Court in November of 1975 when I was sworn in as a justice. When finally announced on January 30, 1976, the opinions resolving those issues in the case of *Buckley* v. *Valeo*[5] totaled 294 pages.

---

5 424 U.S. 1 (1976).

Multiple drafts of those opinions were circulated during the weeks preceding their public release. Although I did not participate in the decision of the case—or in any of the deliberations that preceded the decision—I felt obligated to review what my colleagues were writing and debating. Whether that tedious and seemingly endless reading enhanced my understanding of the subject is a matter of debate, but I do remember acquiring a profound aversion to issues related to the financing of political campaigns while reading those drafts. In order to avoid causing you to share my aversion to the subject, I shall just briefly explain my agreement with Justice Byron White's dissent from a critical portion of the *Buckley* opinion and my reasons for supporting a constitutional amendment to correct the Court's central mistake in that case.

In later years I sometimes agreed and sometimes disagreed with Byron's views about the law, but I always regarded him as a special friend. I had first met him in Pearl Harbor during World War II. He served as a law clerk to

Chief Justice Fred Vinson in the 1946 term, the year before I clerked for Wiley Rutledge; I was especially proud of the fact that he was the first former clerk to become a justice. He played a significant role in Jack Kennedy's campaign for the presidency, which gave him unique insights into the practical aspects of financing political campaigns. While he joined most of the Court's opinion in the *Buckley* case, he was the sole dissenter from its invalidation of the limitations on campaign expenditures that Congress had enacted.

In *Buckley,* the Court of Appeals for the District of Columbia had upheld the statutory limitations on both contributions and expenditures, reasoning that they were regulations of conduct rather than speech and therefore did not abridge the freedom of speech protected by the First Amendment. My new colleagues on the Supreme Court, however, unanimously agreed that the limitations raised a First Amendment issue because they imposed ceilings on the amount of speech that candidates and their supporters could finance. Statutory limitations on the quantity of speech are less troublesome than limitations based on the content of speech and, of course, far less troublesome than limitations based on the viewpoint being expressed in the speech. Thus, even though they merit only what might be described as "third-degree scrutiny" in the hierarchy of First Amendment issues, I agree with the conclusion that such restrictions may violate that amendment if they foreclose too much speech—in the election context, so much so that rival candidates do not have an adequate opportunity to explain to voters why they should win an election.

This conclusion does not require the abandonment of any and all limits on the permissible quantity of speech. The majority of the justices in *Buckley* correctly held that the limitations on contributions were a permissible protection against possible corrupt practices, explaining that there was no evidence that contribution limits "would have any dramatic adverse effect on the funding of campaigns."

But agreement on this point did not mean agreement overall. The majority came to a different conclusion with respect to expenditures. Instead of merely considering the aggregate effect of the ceilings on the campaigns, the majority concluded that they impermissibly prevented wealthy individuals from engaging in some methods of communication. As an example, the majority noted that the limit of $1,000 on individual expenditures would prohibit any individual from purchasing one full-page advertisement in a daily edition of a metropolitan newspaper that charged, as one paper did, $6,971.04 for such an ad. Of course, however, it would not have prevented a group of like-minded voters from chipping in to buy such an ad. And it would have had no effect at all on the many voters who either could not afford — or had no desire — to purchase such an ad.

Whereas the Court's majority focused on the wealthy individual's right to use his own money to affect the outcome of the election, Justice White thought it more important to evaluate the market-wide impact of the limitation. In his view, preventing one speaker from speaking more loudly than others was acceptable as long as the total supply of speech satisfied the voters' demand for information and advice. For him, a ceiling on campaign expenditures "represent[ed] the considered judgment of Congress that elections are to be decided among candidates none of whom has overpowering advantage by reason of a huge campaign war chest. At least so long as the ceiling placed upon the candidates is not plainly too low, elections are not to turn on the difference in the amounts of money that candidates have to spend. This seems an acceptable purpose and the means chosen a common-sense way to achieve it."[6]

But the majority rejected the argument that the "governmental interest in equalizing the relative ability of individuals and groups to influence the outcome of elections serves to justify the limitation on express advocacy...imposed by [the] expenditure ceiling."[7] The Court gave two reasons for such rejection: (1) advocacy of the election or defeat of candidates for federal

---

6 424 U.S. at 265.
7 *Id.* at 48.

office must receive at least as much protection under the First Amendment as the discussion of general policy issues; and (2) "the concept that government may restrict the speech of some elements of our society in order to enhance the relative voice of others is wholly foreign to the First Amendment."

In my judgment, neither of those reasons is correct. On several later occasions the Court has recognized that restrictions on speech seeking to persuade voters to vote for or against a particular candidate may receive less First Amendment protection than speech about other issues. Just two years after the decision in *Buckley,* the Court first held that the First Amendment protected a business corporation's right to spend money to publicize its opposition to a proposed amendment to the Massachusetts Constitution that would have increased its taxes; Justice Lewis Powell in his opinion for the Court explained that "our consideration of a corporation's right to speak on issues of general public interest implies no comparable right in the quite different context of participation in a political campaign for election to public office."[8] And in 1992 the Court upheld a Tennessee statute that silenced all campaign-related speech within 100 feet of a polling place while allowing expression on any other subject, whether religious, commercial, or even political if it was unrelated to issues or candidates being voted upon at the time. In my dissenting opinion, I pointed out that "[c]ampaign-free zones are noteworthy for their broad antiseptic sweep. The Tennessee zone encompasses at least 30,000 square feet around each polling place; in some States, such as Kentucky and Wisconsin, the radius of the restricted zone is 500 feet—silencing an area of over 750,000 square feet."[9]

Even after *Citizens United* the Court handed down a third decision upholding greater restrictions on speech seeking to persuade voters to vote for or against a particular candidate than

8 *First Nat. Bank of Boston* v. *Bellotti,* 435 U.S. 765, 787, n. 26 (1978).

9 See *Burson* v. *Freeman,* 504 U.S. 191, 218 (1992).

on other speech.[10] This was a challenge to the constitutionality of 2 U.S.C. §441e, a federal statute that makes it a crime for anyone who is not an American citizen or a lawful permanent resident to make any contribution to a candidate for federal or state office, or to make any expenditure supporting the election or defeat of any candidate. The two plaintiffs in that third case were aliens lawfully working in the United States — Benjamin Bluman had attended Harvard Law School and was employed by a New York law firm, and Dr. Asenath Steinman was completing her medical residency at Beth Israel Medical Center in New York. Bluman was a Canadian citizen and Steinman was a dual citizen of Canada and Israel. Both of them wanted to spend their own money to advocate the election of certain candidates for federal and state offices, but because neither of them was an American citizen or a lawful permanent resident, they would have committed a federal

---

10 See *Bluman* v. *Federal Election Comm'n,* 132 S. Ct. 1087 (2012).

crime by doing so. In 2011 they brought an action against the Federal Election Commission seeking an injunction against enforcement of Section 441e, contending that the First Amendment, as construed in *Buckley* v. *Valeo* and *Citizens United* v. *Federal Election Commission,* protected their right to do so. (Under *Buckley,* their proposed expenditures qualified as speech of the third degree, and as they read *Citizens United,* the First Amendment prohibited "restrictions distinguishing among different speakers, allowing speech by some but not others.")[11]

A three-judge district court dismissed their complaint. In his thoughtful opinion for the court, Judge Brett Kavanaugh explained that the federal government may exclude foreign citizens from activities "intimately related to the process of democratic self-government."[12] As he read §441e, it "does not restrain foreign nation-

---

11 558 U.S. at 340.

12 *Bluman* v. *Federal Election Comm'n,* 800 F. Supp. 2d 281, 287 (D.D.C. 2011) (*quoting Bernal* v. *Fainter,* 467 U.S. 216, 220 (1984)).

als from speaking out about issues or spending money to advocate their views about issues. It restrains them only from a certain form of expressive activity closely tied to the voting process—providing money for a candidate or spending money in order to expressly advocate for or against the election of a candidate."[13] Judge Kavanaugh then quoted the same excerpt from Justice Powell's 1978 opinion that I included above.

Judge Kavanaugh's reasoning, though entirely correct, was flatly inconsistent with the proposition undergirding the holding by the majority in *Citizens United* that election-related speech by nonvoters is always entitled to at least as much protection under the First Amendment as speech about other issues. The principal authority on which his opinion relied was my dissenting opinion in *Citizens United*.

The same federal statute that gave the plaintiffs the right to have their case heard by a three-judge district court also gave them the right to a

---

13 *Id.* at 290.

direct appeal to the United States Supreme Court. Thus, as a matter of federal law, they were entitled to have the Supreme Court review the merits of the district court's decision. Because the Court has mandatory jurisdiction of such an appeal—unlike its discretionary jurisdiction over most of the petitions for review that make up the bulk of its docket—the Court could not avoid making a decision on the merits. Furthermore, because the district court's decision not only raised a novel and unquestionably important issue but also was inconsistent with a central theme of the majority opinion in *Citizens United*—namely, that a speaker's identity (in that case identity as a corporation) is an impermissible basis for regulating campaign speech—it seemed obvious to me that the Supreme Court would have the case briefed and argued before deciding it. Instead, presumably because it agreed with Judge Kavanaugh's reasoning, the Court unanimously affirmed without filing any opinion at all. That summary affirmance demonstrates that the First Amendment will tolerate *some* regulation of campaign speech that is more restrictive than regulations of speech in other contexts.

As a general matter it is certainly true that speech about controversial policy issues such as gun control or the proper response to global warming may not be censored for the purpose of enhancing the persuasive appeal of either side of the debate. I am not aware of any state or federal laws that have attempted to censor public debate about such issues for that reason. There are, however, situations in which rules limiting the quantity of speech are justified by the interest in giving adversaries an equal opportunity to persuade a decision maker to reach one conclusion rather than another. The most obvious example is an argument before the Supreme Court. Firm rules limit the quantity of both oral and written speech that the parties may present to the decision maker. Those rules assume that the total quantity permitted is sufficient to enable the Court to reach the right conclusion; they are adequately justified by interests in fairness and efficiency.

Those same interests justified rules governing

the conduct of the debates among Republican candidates seeking their party's nomination for president in 2012. It would have been manifestly unfair for the moderator of one of those debates to allow Mitt Romney more time than any other candidate because he had more money than any of his rivals. Restricting his speech "in order to enhance the relative voice of others" made perfect sense, and certainly was not "wholly foreign to the First Amendment." Thus, the *Buckley* majority's second reason for rejecting the interest in equalizing the relative ability of opposing candidates to influence the outcome of elections is entirely unpersuasive.

An unstated third reason must explain the Court's decision—the expenditure limits imposed by the statute under review were too low. Instead of furthering the legitimate interest in providing a level playing field for opposing candidates, they may well have provided incumbents with an unfair advantage. As the Court pointed out, "the equalization of permissible campaign expenditures might serve not to equalize the opportunities of all candidates, but to handicap a candidate who lacked substantial name recognition or exposure of his views before the start of the campaign."[14] Moreover, the *Buckley* majority relied on an earlier decision in *Mills* v. *Alabama*,[15] which invalidated a statute that prohibited newspapers from publishing editorials on election day urging people to vote a certain way on the issues submitted to them. Because the prohibition was based on the content of the speech, it merited stricter scrutiny than a mere limitation on the quantity of speech. The Court in *Mills* held that "no test of reasonableness can save [such] a state law from invalidation as a violation of the First Amendment." After quoting that comment, the *Buckley* Court added: "Yet the prohibition of election-day editorials...is clearly a lesser intrusion on constitutional freedom than a $1,000 limitation on the amount of money any person can spend *during an entire election year* in advocating the election or defeat of a candidate for public office."[16] That

14 424 U.S. at 56–57.
15 384 U.S. 214 (1966).
16 424 U.S. at 51 (emphasis in original).

discussion makes perfect sense as an explanation of why the particular limits imposed by the 1974 statute were too low. But it is not a satisfactory explanation of why all limits on expenditures should be invalid. Nor does it explain why reasonable limits may not level the playing field.

Justice White's position in *Buckley* may have been flawed because he did not squarely confront the question whether the expenditure limits were so low that they may have tipped the scales in favor of incumbents. But he was surely correct in identifying the interest in preventing wealth from becoming the deciding factor in contested elections as valid and significant. I think he was also correct in placing weight on the public's perception of the role of money in influencing the outcome of elections. Voters who believe that the power of the purse will determine the outcome of elections are more likely to become bystanders rather than participants in the political process. Candidates would also benefit by being insulated from the "influence inevitably exerted by the endless job of raising increasingly large sums of money." The advantages of imposing reasonable limits on the amount of money that candidates and their supporters may spend during election campaigns clearly outweigh the disadvantages.

The principal disadvantage that the big spenders identify is a fear that any limit will deprive readers, viewers, and listeners of access to information or arguments that might influence their votes. Their point is valid, but its force diminishes as the volume of speech increases. I believe most members of the television audience share my opinion that at least 75 percent — perhaps even 90 percent — of the campaign commercials could be omitted without depriving viewers of any useful data (indeed, many voters are likely to see the same exact commercial many times in an election cycle). Rather than supporting a prohibition against any limitation on expenditures — no matter how liberal — in my judgment this argument should merely counsel caution against setting limits that are unreasonably low.

I have always found it interesting that in the *Buckley* litigation no one questioned the validity of the total prohibition against campaign expenditures by either corporations or unions that Congress had enacted in 1947 as a part of the Taft-Hartley Act. That total prohibition had expanded the coverage of the earlier statute enacted in response to the statement by President Theodore Roosevelt that I quoted above, which had previously applied only to contributions by corporations.

The validity of the total prohibition on campaign expenditures by either unions or corporations was debated but not decided in 1957 in a case arising out of the prosecution of a union for publishing an editorial in its union newspaper: *United States* v. *Automobile Workers*.[17] In his opinion for the Court, Justice Felix Frankfurter assumed, without squarely deciding, that the prohibition was constitutional. Years later, when the constitutionality of the 1974 Federal Election Campaign Act was debated and decided in

17 352 U.S. 567 (1957).

the *Buckley* litigation, neither the justices nor the parties even mentioned the question whether a ban on corporate expenditures would be permissible. That omission suggests that both the bar and the judiciary assumed that the prohibition against corporate expenditures in the Taft-Hartley Act was perfectly valid. The Michigan state legislature obviously shared that assumption in 1976 when it enacted a statute prohibiting corporations from using corporate treasury funds for independent expenditures in support of, or in opposition to, any candidate in elections for state office. As I have already noted, the validity of that Michigan statute was challenged, and ultimately upheld, in 1990 in *Austin* v. *Michigan Chamber of Commerce.*[18]

In his opinion for the Court, Justice Marshall explained that "the unique state-conferred corporate structure that facilitates the amassing of large treasuries warrants the limit on independent expenditures. Corporate wealth can unfairly influence elections when it is deployed

---

18   494 U.S. 652 (1990).

in the form of independent expenditures, just as it can when it assumes the guise of political contributions."[19] (Of course that comment is equally applicable to wealthy nonresident individuals.) Justices Scalia and Kennedy both wrote dissenting opinions in which they correctly noted that the Court in *Buckley* had rejected the fear of corruption or the interest in equalizing the candidates' opportunity to persuade as permissible justifications for limiting campaign expenditures. But in my judgment that was the central error made by the Court in *Buckley*.

As I noted above, those dissents are especially important because they are the first opinions written by any justice of the Supreme Court expressing the view that corporations have a constitutional right to make unlimited expenditures supporting or opposing candidates in contested elections. Their authors are entitled to credit for persuading three of the eight justices who later joined the Court — Clarence Thomas,

---

19 *Id.* at 660.

John Roberts, and Samuel Alito—to overrule the majority's decision in the Michigan case and to join the opinion in *Citizens United*. (It is somewhat ironic that all of the other five justices who later joined the Court—David Souter, Ruth Ginsburg, Stephen Breyer, Sonia Sotomayor, and Elena Kagan—either joined my dissent in *Citizens United* or have written opinions making it clear that they would have done so had they been on the Court at the time.)

If the Court were to confront the issue decided in the Michigan case today, it would surely comment on the reasoning in Judge Kavanaugh's opinion upholding the ban on campaign expenditures by foreign nationals. That ban did not impose any restriction on their right to speak out in favor of legislative action that would benefit Canadian citizens; it merely limited their ability to influence the selection of the decision makers who would decide whether such legislation should be enacted. The reason Congress excluded them from activities "intimately related to the process of democratic self-government" had nothing to do with the interest in preventing fraud or leveling the playing field. Instead, the statute furthered the federal interest in preserving the power of the voters to control the outcome of elections — an interest that would be impaired if nonvoters had an unlimited right to make campaign expenditures. That federal interest is essentially the same as Michigan's interest, which was protected from impairment by nonvoters' expenditures, in the *Austin* case.

The distinction between debates about issues that legislatures decide and debates during campaigns to elect the members of those legislatures is equally relevant in state and federal elections. The Michigan statute challenged in the 1990 case imposed no restriction on the ability of corporations or any other nonvoters to engage in debates about the wisdom of proposed legislation regulating the use of firearms, as an example, but it did prohibit corporations from making unlimited expenditures in an effort to influence the selection of the officials who decide whether to enact such legislation.

Unlimited expenditures by nonvoters in election campaigns—whether made by nonresidents in state elections or by Canadian citizens, by corporations, by unions, or by trade associations in federal elections—impairs the process of democratic self-government by making successful candidates more beholden to the nonvoters who supported them than to the voters who elected them.

The specific evil that President Roosevelt identified in 1905—"contributing corporate funds to control or aid in controlling elections"—was merely one variety of the threat to the election process that is posed by rules that enhance the power of nonvoters to influence election outcomes. The decision in *Citizens United* took a giant step in the wrong direction. Its most serious consequences can be eliminated without enacting a total prohibition against the use of corporate funds in campaigns. A constitutional amendment authorizing Congress and the states to place "reasonable" limitations on campaign expenditures would allow corporations to make public announcements of their views but would prohibit them from engaging in the kind of repetitive and excessive advocacy that the candidates typically employ. It would also repudiate both the holding and the reasoning in the *Citizens United* case, giving corporations an unlimited right to spend their shareholders' money in election campaigns.

I recognize that reliance on a rule authorizing only reasonable limits on expenditure may invite disputes about the levels selected by Congress. That potential is far less objectionable than the total prohibition against expenditure limits that is the regrettable legacy of *Buckley*. If "reasonableness" is appraised by examining the interests of the entire electorate rather than just the interests of the wealthiest candidates, the issue should not be difficult to resolve. Moreover, a reasonableness threshold would require that the same limit apply to all candidates competing for the same office. I therefore propose this amendment to the Constitution:

Neither the First Amendment nor any other provision of this Constitution shall be construed to prohibit the Congress or any state from imposing reasonable limits on the amount of money that candidates for public office, or their supporters, may spend in election campaigns.

IV

Sovereign Immunity

———◆◇◆———

Unlike the interest in minimizing the risk of catastrophic tragedies and maximizing the efficiency of the federal government's administration of the law that supports the adoption of the amendment proposed in Chapter I, the simple interest in establishing justice provides a sufficient but compelling justification for putting an end to a doctrine that never should have been adopted in a democracy.

In his lecture "The Path of the Law," printed in the *Harvard Law Review* in 1898, Oliver Wendell Holmes made this oft-quoted observation: "It is revolting to have no better reason for a rule of law than that it was so laid down in the time of Henry IV. It is still more revolting if the grounds upon which it was laid down have vanished long since and the rule simply persists from blind imitation of the past."

In 1600, when Henry IV was the king of England, a common-law rule fashioned by judges protected the sovereign from being sued without his consent. Presumably the reason for that rule was a belief that "the king can do no wrong." Or the rule might have been a by-product of the belief that the monarch served by divine right and only God could determine his punishment if he did sin. Not only did those reasons for a rule of sovereign immunity vanish long ago, but it is also clear that neither of them would have been acceptable in America. The recitation in the Declaration of Independence of the abuses committed by George III demonstrates that we never endorsed the first proposition, and the wall between church and state erected by the First Amendment forecloses our endorsement of the second.

To the best of my knowledge, a defense of

sovereign immunity was not raised or discussed in litigation against the colonies or their officials before 1776. Clearly, the colonies were not sovereigns since they were subordinate to the Crown. Indeed, several of their charters expressly authorized suits against them. Moreover, such a doctrine does not appear to have been mentioned at the Constitutional Convention in Philadelphia in 1787. It was, however, a subject of discussion during the ratification process. Opponents of ratification made the argument that the creation of a federal court system would lead to decisions by federal judges requiring the states to pay their war debts. In the Federalist Papers, instead of responding by pointing out that such decisions might well be entirely just, Alexander Hamilton argued that the common-law defense of sovereign immunity, which represented "the general sense and the general practice of mankind," would protect the states from that risk. At Virginia's ratifying convention John Marshall and James Madison made the same point.

As it turned out, Hamilton's prediction was

proved wrong by the Supreme Court's 1793 decision in *Chisholm* v. *Georgia*.[1] In that case, a citizen of South Carolina brought a common-law action against the state of Georgia to recover the $169,000 purchase price of military supplies that had been sold to it during the American Revolution. Four of the five justices who participated in the case concluded that the doctrine of sovereign immunity was not available as a defense. One of those four, Chief Justice John Jay, was an author of the Federalist Papers, and a second, James Wilson, had been one of Pennsylvania's delegates to the Constitutional Convention. Justice James Iredell dissented because, like Hamilton, he believed that sovereign immunity was a well-established common-law defense that Congress had not modified. His argument that Congress should recognize a common-law defense was, of course, quite different from an argument that the Constitution required that result.

Two years later the states reacted to *Chisholm*

---

1 2 U.S. (2 Dall.) 419 (1793).

by ratifying the Eleventh Amendment, which provides that the "Judicial power of the United States" does not extend to suits in which a state is sued by a citizen of another state. The amendment does not mention the doctrine of sovereign immunity or the states' obligation to pay their debts. Instead, it eliminated one of the two sources of federal jurisdiction in actions against state defendants. Article III of the Constitution provides that the federal courts have jurisdiction in "diversity" cases — those brought by a citizen of one state against a citizen of another state — and "federal question" cases — those involving a question of federal law. While the Eleventh Amendment, protects states from being sued by noncitizens in diversity cases, it says nothing about suits raising federal questions.

The two principal opinions discussing the Eleventh Amendment during the years between its ratification in 1795 and the Civil War were both written by Chief Justice John Marshall. In a case decided in 1821, he succinctly explained that the text of the amendment made it clear that "its motive was not to maintain the sovereignty of a State from the degradation supposed to attend a compulsory appearance before the tribunal of the nation" because it preserved federal jurisdiction over states in cases other than those filed by a citizen of another state. "We must ascribe the amendment, then, to some other cause than the dignity of a State. There is no difficulty in finding the cause. Those who were inhibited from commencing a suit against a State . . . were persons who might probably be its creditors." The same mundane purpose that had motivated critics of Article III of the Constitution before it was ratified motivated the states' adoption of the Eleventh Amendment. They did not want federal judges telling them that they had to pay their bills.

Three years later, John Marshall wrote the opinion in *Osborn* v. *Bank of United States*,[2] a landmark case holding that Ohio could not impose a state tax on a national bank. Osborn, an agent of the state, had possession of the tax proceeds, and therefore was able to comply with

---

2 22 U.S. 738 (1824).

a court decree ordering their return to the bank. Marshall's opinion rejected the argument that the suit was barred by the Eleventh Amendment. He severely limited the coverage of the amendment by holding that it applied only to suits in which the state was the party of record, and did not foreclose actions against officials who could provide the relief requested by the plaintiff.

That interpretation of the Eleventh Amendment was followed by the Supreme Court consistently until after the Civil War, most notably in its unanimous decision in 1876, in *Board of Liquidation* v. *McComb*.[3] In that case the Court rebuffed an attempt by Louisiana to modify the terms of a bond issue that had been authorized by a Republican administration, explaining that a state officer could not rely on an unconstitutional act to justify a violation of the plaintiff's rights: "An unconstitutional law will be treated by the courts as null and void."

In sum, during our first century as a sovereign

---

3 92 U.S. 531 (1876).

nation, this comment by Abraham Lincoln in his 1861 State of the Union Address also summarized the prevailing view of John Marshall and the federal judiciary: "It is as much the duty of Government to render prompt justice against itself, in favor of its citizens, as it is to administer the same between private individuals."

During the years immediately after the Civil War constitutional amendments, statutes enacted by a Republican Congress, and executive decisions made by President Ulysses S. Grant dramatically enhanced federal protection for individual rights while curtailing state prerogatives in important respects. Slavery was abolished by the Thirteenth Amendment, which Congress had proposed under President Lincoln's leadership and which the United States ratified in December of 1865. The next year Congress enacted the Civil Rights Act of 1866 over President Andrew Johnson's veto, and two years later the ratification of the Fourteenth Amendment granted citizenship to the former slaves and imposed a duty on the states to provide them with the equal protection of the law. During the administration of President Grant, the federal government was especially active in protecting the new citizens' right to vote. While he was in office, the Fifteenth Amendment, which protects that right from discrimination "on account of race, color, or previous condition of servitude," was ratified, Congress enacted the Ku Klux Klan Act, which still provides the jurisdictional basis for most federal litigation raising constitutional issues, and federal troops were maintained at strategic locations in the South to protect the right to vote. Under this legislation, in the early years of Grant's administration, federal attorneys obtained almost six hundred convictions of members of the Ku Klux Klan, primarily in South Carolina and Alabama. At that time the lower federal courts interpreted the amended Constitution to authorize prosecutions of persons engaged in mass violence against blacks, not only when the police participated in the actual killings—as they did in the New Orleans riot on July 30, 1866—but also when the racists acted independently, as they did when white Klansmen murdered sixty-two blacks in the infamous Colfax Massacre in Grant Parish, Louisiana, on April 13, 1873.

President Grant's decision to maintain a strong military presence in the South, both to combat Klan violence and to protect the former slaves' right to vote, enabled the Republicans to control the state government in Louisiana for several years. In 1868, that government enacted laws prohibiting discrimination in public transportation, authorizing the education of both white and black students in integrated public schools, and regulating slaughterhouses to end a major cause of the pollution in the Mississippi River.

Following the stock market collapse in 1873, and presumably aided by an interest in supporting economic recovery in the South, the Democrats won a majority of the seats in Congress in the 1874 election. In 1876 Samuel Tilden, the Democratic candidate for president, won a majority of the popular vote in an election that was ultimately settled by a compromise that

Exhibit 1

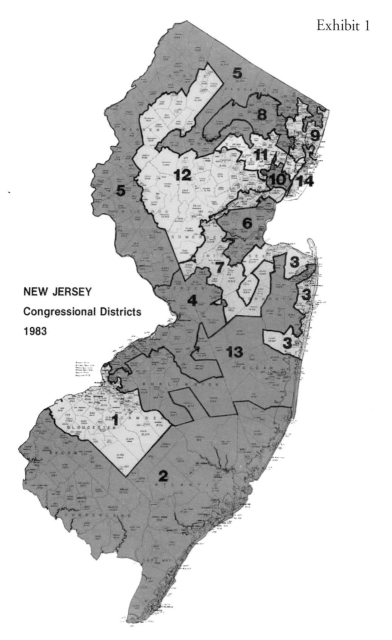

The 1983 New Jersey congressional map. See *Karcher* v. *Daggett*, 462 U.S. 725, 744 (1983).

(This map and those that follow are reproduced as they appear in the U.S. Reports. Although the names of some cities and towns are unclear, each map accurately reflects the important issue in those cases: the "uncouth" shapes of the districts.)

Exhibit 2

APPENDIX A TO OPINION OF O'CONNOR, J.

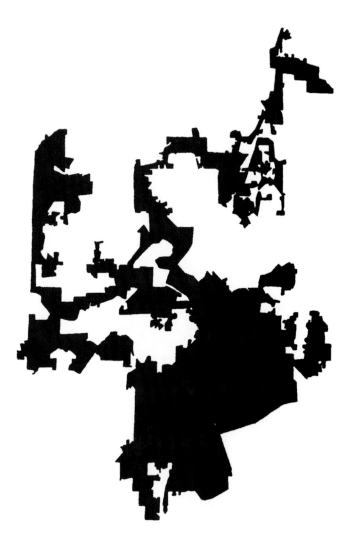

TEXAS CONGRESSIONAL DISTRICT 30

Texas Congressional District 30, enacted in 1991. See *Bush* v. *Vera,* 517 U.S. 952, 987 (1996).

Exhibit 3

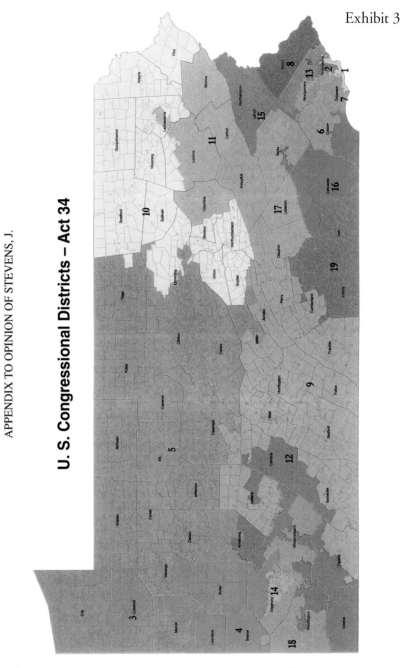

APPENDIX TO OPINION OF STEVENS, J.

U. S. Congressional Districts – Act 34

The 2002 Pennsylvania congressional map. See *Veith* v. *Jubelirer,* 541 U.S. 267, 342 (2004).

Thurgood Marshall, who was appointed by Lyndon Johnson in 1967 and retired in 1991, wrote the Court's opinion in *Puerto Rico* v. *Branstad*, overruling the pre–Civil War case *Kentucky* v. *Dennison*. In that case Chief Justice Taney had held that the federal government could not require a state governor to comply with an order to return a fugitive slave. *(Robert Oakes, Collection of the Supreme Court of the United States)*

Harry Blackmun, who was appointed by Richard Nixon in 1970 and served on the Court until 1994, wrote the Court's opinion in *Garcia* v. *San Antonio Metropolitan Transit Authority*, overruling the Court's 1976 decision in *National League of Cities* v. *Usery*, which invalidated an act of Congress that required the states to comply with the Fair Labor Standards Act. *(Robert Oakes, Collection of the Supreme Court of the United States)*

Felix Frankfurter, who was appointed by Franklin D. Roosevelt in 1939 and retired in 1962, wrote the opinion striking down a racial gerrymander in *Gomillion* v. *Lightfoot*. *(Harris and Ewing Studio, Collection of the Supreme Court of the United States)*

William J. Brennan Jr., who was appointed by Dwight D. Eisenhower in 1956 and retired in 1990, wrote the landmark opinion in *Baker* v. *Carr,* upholding a voter's right to challenge a Tennessee statute under the Fourteenth Amendment's Equal Protection Clause. *(Robert Oakes, Collection of the Supreme Court of the United States)*

Lewis F. Powell Jr., who was appointed by Richard Nixon in 1972 and retired in 1987, wrote the dissenting opinion in *Davis* v. *Bandemer.* He argued that courts should look to a "number of neutral factors" to determine whether a district is an impermissible political gerrymander. *(Robert Oakes, Collection of the Supreme Court of the United States)*

Byron White, who was appointed by John F. Kennedy in 1962 and retired in 1993, was the only justice to dissent from the Court's 1975 decision in *Buckley* v. *Valeo* to invalidate statutory limitations on campaign expenditures. *(Joe Bailey, Collection of the Supreme Court of the United States)*

Brett Kavanaugh, who has been a circuit judge on the United States Court of Appeals for the District of Columbia Circuit since his appointment by George W. Bush in 2006, wrote the opinion for the three-judge district court in *Bluman* v. *Federal Election Comm'n*, upholding the constitutionality of a federal statute making it a crime for anyone who is not an American citizen or a lawful permanent resident to make any expenditure supporting the election or defeat of any candidate for public office. *(Official court photograph, United States Court of Appeals for the District of Columbia Circuit)*

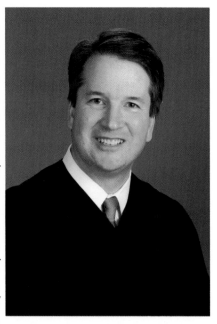

John Marshall, the "Great Chief Justice" from 1801 to 1835, wrote the opinion for the Court in *Osborn* v. *Bank of the United States*. In that case the Court held that Ohio could not impose a tax on the National Bank, and that the Eleventh Amendment did not prevent the Court from ordering state agents to return the tax proceeds because the state itself was not a party to the case. *(John Martin, Collection of the Supreme Court of the United States)*

Ruth Bader Ginsburg, who was appointed by William Jefferson Clinton in 1993, wrote the Court's unanimous opinion in *Florida* v. *Nixon*. That case concerned a lawyer who acknowledged his client's guilt during trial but advised the jury that at the penalty phase of the trial he would introduce evidence showing that his client's conduct was the product of mental illness. Justice Ginsburg's opinion held that such a strategy (without a client's express consent) did not constitute ineffective assistance, and upheld the death sentence. *(Steve Petteway, Collection of the Supreme Court of the United States)*

David Souter, who was appointed by President George H. W. Bush in 1990 and retired in 2009, wrote the dissenting opinion in *Kansas* v. *Marsh*. That five-to-four decision held that the Kansas Supreme Court had erroneously set aside a death sentence because the jury had been instructed that they should impose the death penalty if they concluded in the penalty phase of the trial that the aggravating evidence favoring the death sentence and the mitigating evidence supporting a lesser penalty were in equipoise. *(Joe Bailey, Collection of the Supreme Court of the United States)*

Stephen Breyer, who was appointed by William Jefferson Clinton in 1994, wrote dissenting opinions in *Printz* v. *United States* and *Heller* v. *District of Columbia.* In his dissent in *Printz,* he argued that other federal systems, like Switzerland and Germany, have local states implement regulations and decrees enacted by the central "federal" body. In *Heller,* he argued that laws prohibiting possession of handguns in the home do not violate the Second Amendment. *(Steve Petteway, Collection of the Supreme Court of the United States)*

included an agreement by the Republicans to withdraw all federal troops stationed in the South. Thereafter, the Democratic Party—the party of the Ku Klux Klan—exercised control of all of the state governments in the "Solid South" for decades. In Louisiana a new state constitution, adopted in 1879, repealed the laws enacted in 1868 and expressly repudiated the state's obligation to make payments to holders of bonds issued by the prior administration. A suit brought on behalf of those bondholders brought about a major change in the law.

The plaintiff bondholders in *Louisiana* v. *Jumel*[4] were New York residents. The Supreme Court agreed that they were entitled to payment from tax receipts collected and set aside for the specific purpose of discharging the state's obligations under the bonds. Nevertheless, over the dissents of Justice Stephen Field and the first Justice John Harlan, the Court held that the suit was really against the state and therefore barred by the Eleventh Amendment. The majority

---

4 107 U.S. 711 (1883).

opinion written by Chief Justice Morrison Waite relied primarily on an English precedent, and as both of the dissenters carefully explained, simply rejected the reasoning in John Marshall's pre–Civil War opinions interpreting the Eleventh Amendment.

The timing of the case, and the fact that the Court refused to follow its unanimous decision in the strikingly similar *McComb* case announced in 1868, suggests that the embarrassingly unpersuasive decision reflected the dramatic change in public opinion that had produced a Democratic majority in the country and the withdrawal of federal troops from the South. The lawyer for Louisiana was John Campbell, a former justice of the United States Supreme Court who had been a member of the majority in 1857 in the infamous *Dred Scott* case, which held that blacks could never become citizens; Campbell had resigned from the Court to join the Confederacy. Dissenting Justice Harlan, who was then a junior member of the Court, later became famous for his dissents from majority rulings narrowly construing the Fourteenth Amendment, such as in the

Court's decision invalidating the Civil Rights Act of 1876, and later as the sole dissenter in *Plessy* v. *Ferguson*,[5] the case that upheld the constitutionality of a Louisiana law requiring separate but equal accommodation for nonwhite passengers on trains (and, incidentally, treating a passenger who was seven-eighths Caucasian as nonwhite). In any event, the *Jumel* case marked the beginning of a new era in the Court's sovereign immunity jurisdiction. It was an era of increasing protection for states' rights and decreasing protection for the rights of nonwhites.

A few years later, in *Hans* v. *Louisiana*,[6] which involved another challenge to Louisiana's refusal to pay debts incurred by its Republican administration, the Court followed *Jumel* in holding that the state could not be sued without its consent. The Court viewed the adoption of the Eleventh Amendment as a repudiation of the 1793 decision in *Chisholm* v. *Georgia*[7] and an endorsement of the reasoning in Justice

5 163 U.S. 537 (1896).
6 134 U.S. 1 (1890).
7 2 U.S. (2 Dall.) 419 (1793).

Iredell's dissent in that case. As noted earlier, Justice Iredell reasoned that the common-law doctrine of sovereign immunity had not been modified by Congress and therefore provided a sufficient basis for barring recovery against the state even before the Eleventh Amendment was adopted. Yet the reasoning in Justice Iredell's dissent would not have prevented Congress from modifying or abrogating what he saw as legitimate ancient doctrine either in 1793, when *Chisholm* was decided, or in 1890, when *Hans* v. *Louisiana* was decided.

While the *Hans* case is regarded by many scholars as the principal source of the modern law of sovereign immunity, in my judgment the earlier decision in the *Jumel* case was the real culprit for two reasons: it rejected the limit on the coverage of the Eleventh Amendment announced by John Marshall, and it applied the amendment in a case in which federal jurisdiction should have been upheld because the plaintiffs were asserting a federal right to protection from a state's impairment of their contracts. In both *Jumel* and *Hans* the Court allowed Louisiana to assert a sovereign immunity defense in a case not covered by the Eleventh Amendment.

In both of those cases the Court dealt with the kind of issue that, in Marshall's view, had animated the adoption of the amendment; namely, the state's interest in avoiding payments due to its creditors. The Court made no attempt in either case to explain why the rule was wise or just. Instead, in *Hans* the Court concluded its opinion with a paragraph that might have inspired Holmes's comment about rules dating from the era of Henry IV:

It is not necessary that we should enter upon an examination of the reason or expediency of the rule which exempts a sovereign state from prosecution in a court of justice at the suit of individuals. This is fully discussed by writers on public law. It is enough for us to declare its existence. The legislative department of a state represents its polity and its will, and is called upon by the highest demands of natural and political law to preserve justice and judgment, and to hold inviolate the public obligations. Any departure from this rule, except for reasons most cogent, (of which the legislature, and not the courts, is the judge,) never fails in the end to incur the odium of the world, and to bring lasting injury upon the State itself. But to deprive the legislature of the power of judging what the honor and safety of the state may require, even at the expense of a temporary failure to discharge the public debts, would be attended with greater evils than such failure can cause.

In sum, if the compromise that led to the withdrawal of Union troops allowed the Southern states "to incur the odium of the world" by permitting lynchings and Klan violence to prevent African Americans from voting and to maintain white supremacy, the incremental odium flowing from refusing to pay their debts need not trouble federal judges. The resurrection of the doctrine of state sovereign immunity in the post-Reconstruction years, to use Thurgood

Marshall's language quoted in Chapter I, should not be "representative of the law today."

————

During the decades between the withdrawal of Union troops from the South in 1877 and President Nixon's appointment of William H. Rehnquist to the Supreme Court in 1972, the judge-made sovereign immunity defense was applied in several cases not described in the text of the Eleventh Amendment—for example, a suit brought by the Principality of Monaco seeking recovery from Mississippi on defaulted bonds and an admiralty proceeding brought by the owner of a barge damaged by a vessel owned by the state of New York—but I am quite sure the defense was never even raised in any case seeking recovery against a state or its agents for the violation of an act of Congress.

The defense was, however, raised by the United States in a case decided in 1882 involving the ownership of the land in Virginia where the Arlington National Cemetery is located. The two opinions in that case, which rejected the defense by a five-to-four vote, may well be the most scholarly discussion of the defense contained in the U.S. Reports. I am sure that few of the thousands of tourists who have visited the cemetery are familiar with the history of the case.

The tract of land of about eleven hundred acres had been owned by George Washington Parke Custis, the adopted son of President Washington; Custis executed a will devising a life estate to his daughter, who in 1831 became the wife of a young army officer named Robert E. Lee in a marriage ceremony conducted in the "Custis-Lee Mansion" on the premises. At the expiration of the life estate, her son George W. P. C. Lee acquired ownership of the property. While the elder Lee was commanding the Confederate armies during the Civil War, Congress enacted a statute imposing a new tax on properties in the "insurrectionary districts within the United States," which, of course, included the younger Lee's Arlington estate.

The tax on the property not having been paid, the commissioners appointed under the

federal statute held a sale at which they purchased the property on behalf of the United
States. Lee challenged the validity of the tax
deed in an action filed against two federal officials, Kaufman and Strong, in a Virginia court,
but the case was promptly removed to the federal court, where the attorney general filed a
motion advising the Court that the property in
controversy had been occupied by the United
States, through its officers and agents, for over
ten years as a military station and national cemetery for the burial of deceased soldiers and sail-
ors, and requesting that the suit be dismissed.
The motion did not take any position on the
validity of the tax deed. The judge denied the
motion and held a trial at which the jury concluded that the tax deed was invalid because the
agents of the plaintiff had tried to pay the tax,
but the commissioners had insisted that Lee
make the payment himself.

Even though the United States was not a
party to the trial court proceedings, it prosecuted an appeal in its own name, as did the two
individual defendants. Their appeal raised two

questions: (1) whether any action could be maintained against the United States even if the plaintiff had a clear right to possession of the property; and (2) was Lee's title to the property divested by the tax sale. In his opinion for the Court, Justice Samuel Miller began by discussing the second issue because the Court was unanimous in its agreement with the jury's verdict. The more significant part of his opinion is his explanation of the Court's rejection of the argument that the United States cannot be lawfully sued without its consent in any case, and no action can be maintained against any individual without such consent where the judgment must depend on the right of the United States to property held by such persons as officers or agents of the government. He relied primarily on Justice Marshall's earlier opinion in the *Osborn* case. The importance and relevance of his reasoning justify quoting him at length:

> What is right as established by the verdict of the jury in this case? It is the right to the possession of the homestead of

plaintiff. A right to recover that which has been taken from him by force and violence, and detained by the strong hand. This right being clearly established, we are told that the court can proceed no further, because it appears that certain military officers, acting under the orders of the President, have seized this estate, and converted one part of it into a military fort and another into a cemetery.

It is not pretended, as the case now stands, that the President had any lawful authority to do this, or that the legislative body could give him any such authority except upon payments of just compensation. The defence stands here solely upon the absolute immunity from judicial inquiry of every one who *asserts* authority from the executive branch of the government, however clear it may be made that the executive possessed no such power. Not only no such power is given, but it is absolutely prohibited, both to the executive and the legislative, to deprive any one

131

of life, liberty, or property without due process of law, or to take private property without just compensation.

These provisions for the security of the rights of the citizen stand in the Constitution in the same connection and upon the same ground, as they regard his liberty and his property. It cannot be denied that both were intended to be enforced by the judiciary as one of the departments of the government established by that Constitution....

No man in this country is so high that he is above the law. No officer of the law may set that law at defiance with impunity. All the officers of the government, from the highest to the lowest, are creatures of the law, and are bound to obey it.

It is the only supreme power in our system of government, and every man who by accepting office participates in its functions is only the more strongly bound to submit to that supremacy, and to observe the limitations which it imposes upon the exercise of the authority which it gives.

Courts of justice are established, not only to decide upon the controverted rights of the citizens as against each other, but also upon rights in controversy between them and the government; and the docket of this court is crowded with controversies of the latter class.

Shall it be said, in the face of all this, and the acknowledged right of the judiciary to decide in proper cases, statutes which have been passed by both branches of Congress and approved by the President to be unconstitutional, that the courts cannot give a remedy when the citizen has been deprived of his property by force, his estate seized and converted to the use of the government without lawful authority, without process of law, and without compensation, because the President has ordered it and his officers are in possession?

If such be the law of this country, it sanctions a tyranny which has no existence in the monarchies of Europe, nor in any other government which has a just claim to well-regulated liberty and the protection of personal rights.[8]

Not only did the Court firmly reject the sovereign immunity defense when it was asserted by the federal government to defend action that violated federal law, but it also rejected the defense in 1908 when it was raised by the attorney general of Minnesota in *Ex parte Young*,[9] a case in which a federal court enjoined him from enforcing a newly enacted state statute regulating railroad rates. Citing John Marshall's opinion in the *Osborn* case, the Court explained: "If the act which the state attorney general seeks to enforce be a violation of the Federal Constitution, the officer, in proceeding under such enactment, comes into conflict with the superior

---

8 *United States* v. *Lee*, 106 U.S. 219–221 (1882).
9 209 U.S. 123 (1908).

authority of that Constitution, and he is in that case stripped of his official or representative character and is subjected in his person to the consequences of his individual conduct. The state has no power to impart to him any immunity from responsibility to the supreme authority of the United States." That opinion seemed to make it clear that state officials could not rely on the doctrine of sovereign immunity to defend conduct that violated the federal Constitution. That understanding of the doctrine was accepted for the ensuing sixty-six years.

But in 1974, Justice Rehnquist dramatically expanded the reach of the sovereign immunity defense in his opinion in *Edelman* v. *Jordan*.[10] In that case the district court had held that Illinois had not complied with federal law in administering aid to aged, blind, and disabled persons, and ordered not only strict compliance with federal standards in the future, but also payment of benefits that should have been made in the past. The Court of Appeals, relying on *Ex*

---

10 415 U.S. 651 (1974).

parte Young, also rejected the state's sovereign immunity defense, but the Supreme Court, while affirming the award of prospective relief, held that insofar as private parties—in this case, the class of aged, blind, and disabled persons identified in the statute—seek to impose a liability for past violations of federal law that must be paid from public funds, their claim is barred by the Eleventh Amendment.

Four justices dissented. Justice William O. Douglas correctly pointed out that the Court had recently affirmed four judgments granting retroactive relief against states that had violated federal statutes and that there was no constitutional or policy justification for not applying the reasoning in *Ex parte Young* to retroactive as well as prospective relief. Justice William Brennan also correctly argued that the Eleventh Amendment merely bars suits against states by citizens of other states, and that in the plan of the Constitutional Convention the states had surrendered their sovereign immunity with respect to laws enacted by Congress pursuant to specifically enumerated powers. Justices Thurgood Marshall and Harry Blackmun believed that Illinois had waived its Eleventh Amendment defense by voluntarily participating in the joint federal-state program.

Two years later, in another opinion authored by Justice Rehnquist, the Court adopted what I have always regarded as a rather bizarre limitation on the scope of the sovereign immunity defense. In *Fitzpatrick* v. *Bitzer,*[11] the Court decided that Congress could abrogate the Eleventh Amendment. It allowed employees of the state of Connecticut to recover an award of damages based on the state's violation of Title VII of the Civil Rights Act as amended in 1972; that amendment had added state employees to the class of persons protected against employment discrimination. When Congress enacted the 1972 statute it had expressly relied on both the Commerce Clause and Section 5 of the Fourteenth Amendment, which provides that "Congress shall have power to enforce, by appropriate legislation, the provisions of this article."

---

11 427 U.S. 445 (1976).

In his opinion for the Court Justice Rehnquist relied on that language to support the conclusion that "appropriate legislation" could include actions against states enforcing the Fourteenth Amendment that would be constitutionally impermissible in other contexts; in other words, in appropriate cases Congress could abrogate the Eleventh Amendment. I did not join the Rehnquist opinion for three reasons. First, Connecticut's statutory violation was not also a violation of the Fourteenth Amendment: second, since the Commerce Clause gave Congress ample authority to enact the 1972 statutory amendment, there was no need to consider the relevance of the Fourteenth Amendment to the case; and third, I did not—and still do not—understand how Congress, by enacting a statute, could nullify any part of the Constitution. Nevertheless, ever since 1976, when it decided the *Fitzpatrick* case, the Court has adhered to the view that Congress has the power to abrogate the Eleventh Amendment when enacting legislation to enforce the Fourteenth Amendment.

In sum, those two decisions announced two new rules of constitutional law. *Edelman* limited the rule announced in *Ex parte Young* to awards of prospective relief against states violating the federal Constitution, and held *for the first time* that the Eleventh Amendment barred the recovery of damages from a state violating a federal statute. And *Fitzpatrick* held that Congress could abrogate a provision in the Constitution — namely, the Eleventh Amendment — in legislation enacted to enforce the Fourteenth Amendment.

In later cases the Court narrowed the application of the *Fitzpatrick* exception for federal statutes enacted pursuant to Section 5 of the Fourteenth Amendment by imposing a requirement that the congressional intent to abrogate the Eleventh Amendment defense must be clearly expressed in the statute itself — a requirement, by the way, that would not have been satisfied in the *Fitzpatrick* case itself. Thus, in *Atascadero State Hospital* v. *Scanlon*,[12] the Court

---

12 473 U.S. 234 (1985).

of Appeals had rejected an Eleventh Amendment defense to a claim by a job applicant that the hospital's refusal to hire him because he was partially blind violated the Rehabilitation Act of 1973. The general language in the text of the statute was broad enough to include state hospitals as well as private hospitals, and the legislative history made it perfectly clear that Congress intended to authorize the suit. Nevertheless, in a five-to-four decision in 1985 the Court announced a new rule that trumped the intent of Congress; it stated that "Congress may abrogate the States' constitutionally secured immunity from suit only by making its intention unmistakably clear in the language of the statute."[13]

Congress responded to the *Atascadero* decision by amending a number of statutes. Typically those amendments were uncontroversial and merely stated explicitly what Congress thought its existing legislation had already provided. So, for example, in 1992 Congress

---

13 *Id.* at 242 (1985).

enacted two separate statutes to clarify and confirm its intent to authorize suits against states for patent infringement and trademark infringement. Both of those statutes had been approved by unanimous votes in both houses of Congress; the report of the Senate Judiciary Committee recommending their enactment explained that they were patterned after a statute enacted in 1989 to clarify Congress's intent to authorize suits against states for copyright infringement. Furthermore, the Senate committee report on the Copyright Remedy Clarification Act explained that it was enacted in response to the Court's *Atascadero* decision. The report explained that legislative history made it "absolutely clear" that in 1976 Congress intended to make states fully liable for copyright infringement, and that the Copyright Office was convinced "that copyright proprietors have demonstrated that they will suffer immediate harm if they are unable to sue infringing states in federal court." Accordingly, Congress provided a reasonable explanation for its decisions in 1976 and again in 1989 to authorize suits against sovereign states for copyright infringement. State agencies violating federal law should receive the same treatment as private entities guilty of violating the same laws. The House report on the two 1992 statutes similarly explained that they were enacted in response to the Court's 1985 clear statement requirement. That report confirmed that Congress not only thought that the states should be liable for patent infringement and trademark infringement in 1999, but also that earlier Congresses had reached the same conclusion when they enacted the Copyright Act of 1976 and when they amended the patent code in 1992.

Put simply, Congress had made essentially the same decision with respect to the liability of states for violating federal laws protecting intellectual property on at least five different occasions. Those decisions not only had bipartisan support in both the Senate and the House of Representatives, but also had the approval of the president as well. Moreover, since none of those statutes could even arguably have been enacted to enforce the Fourteenth Amendment, it seems quite clear that the senators and representatives who voted to enact them did not believe that their power to abrogate the sovereign immunity defense was limited to statutes based on that amendment; and rightly so, since there is no sensible reason for imposing any such restriction on Congress.

Yet two cases that followed Congress's decision to subject the states to liability in a range of areas still further expanded the coverage of the sovereign immunity defense. In 1996, in what was unquestionably the most important opinion that Bill Rehnquist wrote during his tenure as chief justice, the five-person majority in *Seminole Tribe of Fla.* v. *Florida*[14] (Chief Justice Rehnquist joined by Justices O'Connor, Scalia, Kennedy, and Thomas) invalidated the Indian Gaming Regulatory Act, which had been enacted in 1988. The act provided that an Indian tribe may conduct certain gaming activities only in conformance with a valid compact between the tribe and the state where the

---

14 517 U.S. 44 (1996).

gambling takes place and imposed upon the states a duty to negotiate in good faith with an Indian tribe seeking such a compact. The statute also authorized a tribe to bring suit in federal court against a state in order to compel performance with that duty. The majority held that notwithstanding Congress's clear intent to abrogate the states' sovereign immunity, it had no power to do so because the statute had been enacted pursuant to the Indian Commerce Clause rather than the Fourteenth Amendment. In one fell swoop, not only the 1988 statute but all of the acts of Congress that had been enacted in response to the *Atascadero* case were invalidated.

In 1999, the same five-person majority (this time Justice Kennedy wrote and was joined by Chief Justice Rehnquist and Justices O'Connor, Scalia, and Thomas) made an even more dramatic change in the law. In *Alden* v. *Maine*,[15] that majority held that the Constitution prohibited Congress from authorizing private litigation

---

15 527 U.S. 706 (1999).

brought by a group of probation officers against the state of Maine to recover damages for violations of the Fair Labor Standards Act, despite the fact that many years ago the Court had held that Congress could require state courts to enforce other federal statutes. In his fifty-five-page opinion for the majority, Justice Kennedy explained that the source of the state's sovereign immunity defense was not the Eleventh Amendment after all, but rather an unwritten rule that was embodied in the "plan of the Convention."

Justice Kennedy's review of the historical materials suggests that he and his four colleagues had a better understanding of the plan of the Convention than John Marshall or the four justices in the majority in the 1793 decision in *Chisholm* v. *Georgia;* indeed, the *Alden* Court went far beyond the argument made by Justice Iredell in his *Chisholm* dissent. The fact that Justice Kennedy cited the *Printz* case (which I discussed in Chapter I) thirteen times adds emphasis to the fact that the rule he announced is totally unsupported by the text of the Constitution.

Congress's power to enact laws that impose obligations on states and state agencies should include the power to authorize effective remedies for violations of those federal commands. The fact that a hospital is owned by a state should not provide it with a sovereign immunity defense to a claimed violation of federal law for which an otherwise identical hospital that is owned by a charity or a municipality would be liable. It is simply unfair to permit state-owned institutions to assert defenses to federal claims that are unavailable to their private counterparts. A university should be equally responsible for copyright or patent infringement whether it is owned privately or by a state. It does not make sense to provide a police officer employed by the state of New York with a defense to a claim that he violated a suspect's constitutional rights that is not available to an officer employed by the city of New York. To avoid such injustices, the Constitution should be amended to provide:

Neither the Tenth Amendment, the Eleventh Amendment, nor any other provision of this Constitution, shall be construed to provide any state, state agency, or state officer with an immunity from liability for violating any act of Congress, or any provision of this Constitution.

V

The Death Penalty

———◦———

During an oral argument in a capital case in the spring of 1982, a man in the audience stood up and started to take off his clothes. His bizarre behavior was intended to dramatize his opposition to the death penalty, but the Supreme Court police removed him so silently and promptly that the argument proceeded without interruption. A few days later my wife, Maryan, and I were guests at a state dinner at the White House. She sat next to Charles Zwick, director of the United States Information Agency (USIA), and I was seated at President Reagan's table next to Queen Beatrix of the

Netherlands. My assumption that my dinner companions would be interested in a description of the unusual protest at the Court could not have been more misguided; as a raconteur, I really laid an egg. Maryan, on the other hand, got along famously with her dinner partner. As a result, we later received an invitation from the USIA to go to Helsinki to represent the United States at a celebration of the fortieth anniversary of an organization formed to maintain friendly relations between Finland and the United States. Shortly after we arrived in Helsinki, our ambassador arranged a press conference with about a dozen representatives of the Finnish news media. The entire conference consisted of variations on one question: "Why does the United States still have the death penalty?" In my repeated attempts to answer that question I must have laid another egg, because it was obvious that none of the reporters were favorably impressed by anything I said to justify that institution.

I had told them that our decisions upholding the constitutionality of state capital punishment statutes did not mean that the justices agreed with the wisdom of the legislation. Indeed, I think Warren Burger and Harry Blackmun — who were both former residents of Minnesota, which did not permit capital punishment — had both stated publicly that as a matter of policy they opposed the death penalty. Rather, the Court had merely held that under our Constitution it was permissible for state legislators to conclude that the possibility of being sentenced to death might deter some potential murderers from committing that crime, and that community outrage sometimes demanded retribution for especially vicious crimes. Intervening events have convinced me that even if the death penalty was justified in 1982, this is no longer the case.

It was after that visit that I learned why the state of Michigan does not have the death penalty. As David Garland explains in his book *Peculiar Institution*, in 1846 the state legislature adopted a statute abolishing capital punishment for any crime other than treason. The sponsors of the legislation were concerned about the "fallibility" of capital punishment. As Professor

Garland explains, an innocent man had recently been executed in Canada, and the state senator who introduced the bill had apparently presided over the execution of an innocent person while serving as a sheriff in New York. Some years later, Michigan lawmakers concluded that the state constitution should be amended to avoid the risk of such an injustice. Over the years since my visit to Finland I have concluded that the federal Constitution should also either be construed or amended to avoid that risk.

The enactment by most state legislatures of statutes authorizing sentences of life imprisonment without the possibility of parole has eliminated one justification for the death penalty and so reduced the significance of another that it barely passes the rational basis test. It can no longer be argued that execution of a potentially dangerous offender is necessary in order to remove the risk that he will commit further crimes. And the notion that the possible imposition of a death sentence is a significant deterrent on potential murderers must be modified to evaluate the marginal difference between the deterrent effect of that possible sentence and the deterrent effect of a sentence of life imprisonment without the possibility of parole. It is unlikely that criminals contemplating vicious crimes engage in the kind of cost-benefit analysis that would draw a distinction between those sentences. The real justification for preserving capital punishment surely rests on the interest in retribution. "An eye for an eye and a tooth for a tooth" provides an explanation for preserving capital punishment that is both more realistic and more acceptable than any other.

That justification is consistent with the repeated decisions of state legislatures to limit the availability of the death sentence to cases in which statutorily defined aggravating circumstances must be proved in order to establish the defendant's eligibility for that penalty. It is also consistent with Justice Potter Stewart's view that "death sentences are cruel and unusual in the same way that being struck by lightning is cruel and unusual.... the Eighth and Fourteenth Amendments cannot tolerate the infliction of a sentence of death under legal systems that permit this unique penalty to be so wantonly and so freakishly imposed."[1] And retribution is surely the only justification for the Supreme Court's shameful approval of the prosecutor's use of so-called victim-impact testimony at the penalty phase of capital cases even when the evidence sheds no light on either the guilt or the moral culpability of the defendant. In sum, I am convinced that the question whether we should retain the death penalty depends on the strength of the interest in retribution — the interest in avenging the harms caused by the most vicious criminals. I shall therefore comment on two cases that shed light on the diminishing importance of that interest, and then conclude with a comment on the finality of the death sentence in a criminal justice system that is not infallible, and an amendment to put an end to what has become a wretched arrangement.

---

1 *Furman* v. *Georgia,* 408 U.S. 238, 309–310 (1972) (Stewart, J., concurring).

On August 12, 1984, Joe Elton Nixon, then twenty-three years old, committed a brutal murder that would have made him eligible for the death penalty in any jurisdiction that authorizes capital punishment. He had approached Jeanne Bickner in a shopping mall, asked her to help him jump-start his car, and then accepted her offer to drive him home. He directed her to drive to a remote location where he overpowered her, tied her to a tree with jumper cables, torched her personal belongings, and used them to set her on fire. Her charred body made it obvious that she had suffered a gruesome, excruciatingly painful death. The police promptly apprehended Nixon and collected overwhelming evidence establishing his guilt. Before his trial, his appointed counsel offered to have him plead guilty in exchange for the prosecutor's recommendation of any sentence other than death. When the prosecutor declined that offer, the only issue that separated the parties was the question whether Nixon would be allowed to die a natural death in prison or be executed by the state. Answering that question in Nixon's case—as in most capital cases—was time consuming and extremely costly for the state of Florida.

In his opening statement Nixon's lawyer, Michael Corin, acknowledged Nixon's guilt but advised the jury that at the penalty phase of the trial he would introduce evidence showing that his client's conduct was the product of mental illness. Nixon himself was excluded from attendance at most of the trial because of his disruptive and violent misbehavior. No evidence was offered on his behalf during the guilt phase. At the penalty phase, however, Corin presented the testimony of eight witnesses, including friends and relatives who described Nixon's emotional troubles and erratic behavior, and both a psychologist and a psychiatrist who addressed his history of emotional instability, his low IQ, and the possibility that he had suffered brain damage. After three hours of deliberation the jury recommended the death sentence, which the trial court imposed.

On direct appeal to the Florida Supreme Court, Nixon's new lawyer argued that Corin had rendered ineffective assistance by conceding Nixon's guilt without his express consent. Given the similarity between that strategy and a guilty plea, and the fact that the law is well settled that counsel may not enter a guilty plea without first obtaining his client's express consent, there was obviously a substantial basis for the argument. (A similar argument had been endorsed by state supreme courts in Illinois and South Carolina, and by the federal Court of Appeals for the Sixth Circuit.) Instead of either approving or disapproving Corin's trial strategy in the direct appeal from Nixon's conviction, the Florida Supreme Court invited him to raise the issue in a state post-conviction proceeding at which a state trial judge could receive whatever further evidence his new lawyer might present. After multiple evidentiary hearings and appeals, in 2003 — nineteen years after the crime — the Florida Supreme Court upheld Nixon's claim because the evidence did not establish that he had made the kind of explicit consent that a valid guilty plea would require.

The elected state attorney general, Charles

Crist—who was later elected governor—then filed a petition for certiorari, presenting the United States Supreme Court with the question whether Nixon had the burden of proving that he was prejudiced by his lawyer's trial strategy. The Court granted the petition and reversed the state supreme court, thus finally ending the litigation. Justice Ginsburg, with her characteristic eloquence, wrote what turned out to be a unanimous opinion. She noted that the renowned advocate Clarence Darrow had "famously employed a similar strategy as counsel for the youthful, cold-blooded killers Richard Loeb and Nathan Leopold."[2]

The fact that Justice Ginsburg was so persuasive in explaining the reasonableness of Corin's trial strategy surely does not raise any question about the competence of the state judges who had come to a different conclusion. Indeed, although I did not agree with my law clerk's analysis in the case, I find this excerpt from his cert memo interesting. He wrote: "I think the

---

2 *Florida* v. *Nixon,* 543 U.S. 175, 192 (2004).

Florida court got it exactly right: While it may on occasion be a legitimate strategy for a lawyer to concede his client's guilt during the guilt phase of a capital trial, the decision to choose such a strategy belongs to the client. When a lawyer pursues such a strategy without a client's consent, that lawyer's actions constitute an impermissible forfeiture of the client's constitutional right to an adversarial proceeding to determine guilt."

The expression of that opinion was fully consistent with his qualifications as a law clerk. Surely the earlier expression of the same opinion by judges on the Florida Supreme Court should not provide a basis for removing them from the bench. Nevertheless, in the judicial retention election in 2012—twenty-eight years after the crime—the political party in control of Florida's government sponsored a campaign to use three justices' votes in the *Nixon* case as a basis for removing them from the court. The campaign was not successful—all three justices won retention by substantial majorities—but it illustrates the fact that the political consequences of death penalty litigation may be more important than vindicating the state's interest in retribution.

The post-conviction litigation in the *Nixon* case was protracted and expensive. Whether those costs were justified depends, I suppose, on the importance of vindicating the state's interest in retribution by putting Nixon to death. Nevertheless, despite the elapse of over eight years from the date of the United States Supreme Court's decision — and over twenty-eight years from the date when the Florida prosecutor rejected the offer of a guilty plea that would have required Nixon to spend the rest of his life in prison — he remains alive on death row today. He has not been on death row as long as Gary Eldon Alvord — who was sentenced to death in 1974 — but the long delay in cases like Nixon's and Alvord's surely demonstrates that it is not necessary to put the defendant to death in order to vindicate the state's interest in obtaining retribution for a heinous crime. (Alvord, for his part, suffers from disordered thinking and delusions, which under the Court's decision forbidding capital punishment of the insane in *Ford* v. *Wainwright*[3] likely make him ineligible for execution. Because the state cannot execute him but also refuses to commute his death sentence, Alvord appears destined to live out the remainder of his natural life under the harsh conditions of death row.)

————

In 2008, in *Baze* v. *Rees*,[4] the Supreme Court upheld the constitutionality of Kentucky's method of executing its prisoners who have been sentenced to death. At the time, the state used a three-step lethal injection procedure similar to that used by the federal government and most other states. The first drug, sodium thiopental, is a barbiturate that makes the prisoner unconscious; the second, pancuronium bromide, causes paralysis; and the third, potassium chloride, causes a fatal heart attack. The purpose of the barbiturate is to prevent the prisoner from feeling the pain caused

————

3 477 U.S. 399 (1986).
4 553 U.S. 35 (2008).

by the second injection. The second does not serve any therapeutic purpose; it is used to preserve the dignity of the procedure by preventing involuntary muscle movements that observers might incorrectly perceive to be convulsions or seizures caused by severe pain. Because it masks any outward sign of distress, pancuronium bromide creates a risk that the inmate will suffer excruciating pain before death occurs.

There is a general understanding among veterinarians that the risk of pain is sufficiently serious that the use of pancuronium bromide should be prohibited when an animal's life is being terminated. As a result of that understanding among knowledgeable professionals, Kentucky, like several other states, has enacted legislation prohibiting the use of the drug in animal euthanasia. The inmate petitioners in the *Baze* case argued that Kentucky should not be permitted to kill them by using a drug that it would not permit to be used on their pets.

The risk that prison personnel may make a mistake that will cause excruciating and undetectable pain is enhanced by the fact that the codes of ethics of the American Medical Association, the American Nurses Association, and the National Association of Emergency Medical Technicians prohibit their members from taking part in executions. Nevertheless, after hearing extensive testimony by experts and by Kentucky corrections officials during a seven-day bench trial, the Kentucky trial judge rejected the inmates' challenge to the constitutionality of the procedure because he was not convinced that it created an unreasonable risk of causing excruciating pain. The Kentucky Supreme Court affirmed, as did the United States Supreme Court. Nevertheless, more recently, Kentucky has announced that it will join Texas, Arizona, Ohio, and seven other states that now use a single-drug regime for executions and employ a single dose of a barbiturate—either sodium thiopental or pentobarbital—in future executions.

Two features of executions in Elizabethan England and lynchings in Texas as late as 1893 served the public interest in retribution: the events were public spectacles that attracted large crowds, and they were designed to inflict excruciating pain before death occurred. The *Baze* case is significant because it dramatically illustrates how our society has moved away from public and painful retribution toward ever more humane forms of punishment. Today, instead of a public spectacle, an execution is almost as private as the administration of anesthesia before an operation in a hospital. The use of pancuronium bromide to paralyze the inmate protects those who do witness the event from possible discomfort from witnessing what might otherwise be perceived as a painful event. More important, the law now prohibits the state from deliberately inflicting any pain at all on the offender.

The dispute in *Baze* was over the factual question whether the state had taken adequate precautions to avoid the risk that improper administration of the three-drug protocol would inadvertently cause pain, not whether it could deliberately do so. The dispute generated seven different opinions by Supreme Court justices, but none suggested that the interest in retribution would allow the state to cause any pain deliberately. Chief Justice Roberts's opinion apparently assumed that a method of execution would violate the Eighth Amendment if it posed a substantial risk of severe pain that could be reduced by adopting readily available alternatives. Justice Clarence Thomas criticized that view as too lenient because in his view the Constitution contains a bright-line rule that merely prohibits any deliberate infliction of pain. But even under his view the interest in retribution would not justify any attempt to apply an "eye for an eye" standard of punishment. Just as the *Nixon* case and its aftermath illustrate the waning public support for using the death penalty to avenge serious crimes, the *Baze* case reminds us that the Court has already developed a rule of law that prohibits states from subjecting the defendant to the kind of pain that he inflicted on his victim.

———

The requirement that guilt of a criminal charge be established by proof beyond a reasonable doubt has been a part of our law from our early years as a nation, but it was not until 1970 that the Court finally held that it was an aspect of "due process" protected by the Fifth and Fourteenth Amendments to the Constitution. *In re Winship*[5] was a case in which a New York family court judge found that a twelve-year-old boy had entered a locker and stolen $112 from a woman's pocketbook. The judge acknowledged that the evidence was not sufficient to establish the boy's guilt beyond a reasonable doubt, but held that that standard of proof did not apply to delinquency proceedings under the New York Family Court Act, even though the finding justified the boy's placement in a training school until he reached his eighteenth birthday.

When the case was reviewed in the United States Supreme Court, the judgment was reversed on the ground that the trial judge should have applied the "proof beyond a reasonable doubt" standard. In his concurring opinion Justice Harlan explained that the requirement of proof

---

5 397 U.S. 358 (1970).

beyond a reasonable doubt in a criminal case is "bottomed on a fundamental value determination of our society that it is far worse to convict an innocent man than to let a guilty man go free."[6] That value determination increases in importance as the severity of the sentence increases.

Despite requiring proof of guilt that satisfies the beyond-a-reasonable-doubt standard, there is general agreement that juries do occasionally make mistakes and convict defendants who are actually innocent. This disturbing conclusion has been confirmed during the period after 1989, when DNA testing became widely available. The large number of exonerations includes a significant number of defendants who had been sentenced to death. Whether any innocent defendants have actually been put to death, and if so how many, are subjects bitterly debated by scholars.

The character of that debate is illustrated by the dissenting opinion of Justice Souter, and the

_____

6 *Id*. at 372.

response by Justice Scalia, in *Kansas* v. *Marsh*.[7] In that case the Kansas Supreme Court had set aside a death sentence because the jury had been instructed that if they concluded in the penalty phase of the trial that the aggravating evidence favoring a death sentence and the mitigating evidence supporting a lesser sentence were in equipoise, the jurors should sentence the defendant to death. By a vote of five to four the U.S. Supreme Court held that the instruction was proper and reversed the judgment of the state supreme court.

In his dissent Justice Souter characterized the instruction that placed "a thumb on death's side of the scale" as "morally absurd" under precedent dating back to 1972, and then included a section discussing "a new body of fact" that must be accounted for in deciding what the Eighth Amendment should tolerate because "the period starting in 1989 has seen repeated exonerations of convicts under death sentences, in numbers never imagined before the develop-

---

7 548 U.S. 163 (2006).

ment of DNA tests."[8] Responding to that dissent, Justice Scalia argued at length that the studies cited by Justice Souter were unreliable and inaccurate. Justice Scalia cited another study in which, for the period between 1989 and 2003, the authors identified "340 'exonerations' *nationwide*—not just for capital cases, mind you, nor even just for murder convictions, but for various felonies." Given the fact that during that period there were more than 15 million felony convictions across the country, the error rate was .027 percent and the success rate was 99.973 percent. Moreover, in his view "*none* of the cases included in the .027 error rate for American verdicts involved a capital defendant erroneously executed."[9]

He then summarized his view of the relevant evidence in these three sentences: "Like other human institutions, courts and juries are not perfect. One cannot have a system of criminal punishment without accepting the possibility

8 *Id.* at 207.
9 *Id.* at 198.

that someone will be punished mistakenly. That is a truism, not a revelation. But with regard to the punishment of death in the current American system, that possibility has been reduced to an insignificant minimum."[10]

For me, the question that cannot be avoided is whether the execution of only an "insignificant minimum" of innocent citizens is tolerable in a civilized society. Given the availability of life imprisonment without the possibility of parole as an alternative method of preventing the defendant from committing further crimes and deterring others from doing so, and the rules that prevent imposing an "eye for an eye" form of retributive punishment, I find the answer to that question pellucidly clear. When it comes to state-mandated killings of innocent civilians, there can be no "insignificant minimum."

In 1846 evidence that two innocent men had been put to death by hanging convinced the Michigan legislature that the criminal justice system is not infallible and that a civilized soci-

---

10 *Id.* at 199.

ety should not preserve a criminal sanction that risks the repetition of such an intolerable injustice. We may never know how many innocent prisoners have actually been put to death. We do know, however, that the risk of such injustice arises whenever a defendant is sentenced to death. Moreover, we also know that the risk is significant and that the finality of state action terminating the life of one of its citizens precludes any possible redress if a mistake does occur.

That risk can, and should, be eliminated by adding five words to the text of the Eighth Amendment, which already prohibits the states as well as the federal government from imposing cruel and unusual punishments. The inclusion of the words "such as the death penalty" in the text of that amendment would make it read:

> Excessive bail shall not be required, nor excessive fines imposed, nor cruel and unusual punishments such as the death penalty inflicted.

VI

The Second Amendment
(Gun Control)

———◄○►———

Concern that the anti-commandeering rule hampers the federal government's ability to obtain adequate databases that will identify persons who should not be permitted to purchase guns prompted my discussion of the importance of doing away with that rule. During the months following the massacre of grammar school children in Newtown, Connecticut, high-powered automatic weapons have been used to kill innocent victims in more senseless public incidents. Those killings, however, are only a fragment of the total harm caused by the misuse of firearms.

Each year over 30,000 people die in the United States in firearm-related incidents. Many of those deaths involve handguns.

The adoption of rules that will lessen the number of those incidents should be a matter of primary concern to both federal and state legislators. Legislatures are in a far better position than judges to assess the wisdom of such rules and to evaluate the costs and benefits that rule changes can be expected to produce. It is those legislators, rather than federal judges, who should make the decisions that will determine what kinds of firearms should be available to private citizens, and when and how they may be used. Constitutional provisions that curtail the legislative power to govern in this area unquestionably do more harm than good.

The first ten amendments to the Constitution placed limits on the powers of the new federal government. Concern that a national standing army might pose a threat to the security of the separate states led to the adoption of the Second Amendment, which provides "A well regulated Militia, being necessary to the security of a free

State, the right of the people to keep and bear Arms, shall not be infringed."

For over two hundred years following the adoption of that amendment federal judges uniformly understood that the right protected by that text was limited in two ways: first, it applied only to keeping and bearing arms for military purposes, and second, while it limited the power of the federal government, it did not impose any limit whatsoever on the power of states or local governments to regulate the ownership or use of firearms. Thus, in *United States* v. *Miller*,[1] decided in 1939, the Court unanimously held that Congress could prohibit the possession of a sawed-off shotgun because that sort of weapon had no reasonable relation to the preservation or efficiency of a "well regulated Militia." When I joined the Court in 1975, that holding was generally understood as limiting the scope of the Second Amendment to uses of arms that were related to military activities. During the years when Warren Burger was chief justice, from

---

1 307 U.S. 174 (1939).

1969 to 1986, no judge or justice expressed any doubt about the limited coverage of the amendment, and I cannot recall any judge suggesting that the amendment might place any limit on state authority to do anything. Organizations like the National Rifle Association disagreed with that position and mounted a vigorous campaign claiming that federal regulation of the use of firearms severely curtailed Americans' Second Amendment rights. Five years after his retirement, during a 1991 appearance on the *MacNeil/Lehrer NewsHour,* Burger himself remarked that the Second Amendment "has been the subject of one of the greatest pieces of fraud, I repeat the word 'fraud,' on the American public by special interest groups that I have ever seen in my lifetime."

In recent years two profoundly important changes in the law have occurred. In 2008, by a vote of five to four, the Court decided in *District of Columbia* v. *Heller*[2] that the Second Amendment protects a civilian's right to keep a hand-

___
2 554 U.S. 570 (2008).

gun in his home for purposes of self-defense. And in 2010, by another vote of five to four, the Court decided in *McDonald* v. *Chicago*[3] that the Due Process Clause of the Fourteenth Amendment limits the power of the city of Chicago to outlaw the possession of handguns by private citizens. I dissented in both of those cases and remain convinced that both decisions misinterpreted the law and were profoundly unwise. Public policies concerning gun control should be decided by the voters' elected representatives, not by federal judges.

In my dissent in the *McDonald* case, I pointed out that the Court's decision was unique in the extent to which the Court had exacted a

> heavy toll in terms of state sovereignty... even apart from the States' long history of firearms regulation and its location at the core of their police powers, this is a quintessential area in which federalism ought to be allowed to flourish

---

3 130 S.Ct. 3020 (2010).

without this Court's meddling. Whether or not we *can* assert a plausible constitutional basis for intervening, there are powerful reasons why *we should not* do so.

Across the Nation, States and localities vary significantly in the patterns and problems of gun violence, as well as in the traditions and cultures of lawful gun use.... The City of Chicago, for example, faces a pressing challenge in combatting street gangs. Most rural areas do not.[4]

In response to the massacre of grammar school students at Sandy Hook Elementary School on December 14, 2012, some legislators have advocated stringent controls on the sale of assault weapons and more complete background checks on purchasers of firearms. It is important to note that nothing in either the *Heller* or the *McDonald* opinion poses any obstacle to the adoption of such preventive measures. First, the Court did not overrule *Miller*. Instead, it "read

---

4 130 S.Ct. at 3114.

Miller to say only that the Second Amendment does not protect those weapons not typically possessed by law-abiding citizens for lawful purposes, such as short-barreled shotguns."[5] On the preceding page of its opinion, the Court had made it clear that even though machine guns were useful in warfare in 1939, they were not among the types of weapons protected by the Second Amendment because that protected class was limited to weapons in common use for lawful purposes like self-defense. Even though a sawed-off shotgun or a machine gun might well be kept at home and be useful for self-defense, neither machine guns nor sawed-off shotguns satisfy the "common use" requirement. Thus, even as generously construed in *Heller,* the Second Amendment provides no obstacle to regulations prohibiting the ownership or use of the sorts of automatic weapons used in the tragic multiple killings in Virginia, Colorado, and Arizona in recent years. The failure of Congress to take any action to minimize the risk of

---

5 554 U.S. at 625.

similar tragedies in the future cannot be blamed on the Court's decision in *Heller*.

A second virtue of the opinion in *Heller* is that Justice Scalia went out of his way to limit the Court's holding not only to a subset of weapons that might be used for self-defense, but also to a subset of conduct that is protected. The specific holding of the case only covers the possession of handguns in the home for purposes of self-defense, while a later part of the opinion adds emphasis to the narrowness of that holding by describing uses that were not protected by the common law or state practice. Prohibitions on carrying concealed weapons, on the possession of firearms by felons and the mentally ill, and laws forbidding the carrying of firearms in sensitive places such as schools and government buildings or imposing conditions and qualifications on the commercial sale of arms are specifically identified as permissible regulations.[6]

---

6 554 U.S. at 626–627.

Thus, Congress's failure to enact laws that would expand the use of background checks and limit the availability of automatic weapons cannot be justified by reference to the Second Amendment or to anything that the Supreme Court has said about that amendment. What the members of the five-justice majority said in those opinions is nevertheless profoundly important, because they curtail the government's power to regulate the use of handguns that contribute to the roughly eighty-eight firearm-related deaths that occur every day.

There is an intriguing similarity between the Court's sovereign immunity jurisprudence, which began with a misinterpretation of the Eleventh Amendment, and its more recent misinterpretation of the Second Amendment. As I explained in Chapter IV, the procedural amendment limiting federal courts' jurisdiction over private actions against states eventually blossomed into a substantive rule that treats the common-law doctrine of sovereign immunity as though it were part of the Constitution itself.

Of course, in England common-law rules fashioned by judges may always be repealed or amended by Parliament. And when the United States became an independent nation, the Congress and every state legislature had the power to accept, to reject, or to modify common-law rules that prevailed prior to 1776, except, of course, any rule that might have been included in the Constitution. The Second Amendment expressly endorsed the substantive common-law rule that protected the citizen's right (and duty) to keep and bear arms when serving in a state militia. In its decision in *Heller,* however, the majority interpreted the amendment as though its draftsmen were primarily motivated by an interest in protecting the common-law right of self-defense. But that common-law right is a procedural right that has always been available to the defendant in criminal proceedings in every state. The notion that the states were concerned about possible infringement of that right by the federal government is really quite absurd.

As a result of the rulings in *Heller* and *McDonald,* the Second Amendment, which was adopted to protect the states from federal interference with their power to ensure that their militias were "well regulated," has given federal judges the ultimate power to determine the validity of state regulations of both civilian and militia-related uses of arms. That anomalous result can be avoided by adding five words to the text of the Second Amendment to make it unambiguously conform to the original intent of its draftsmen. As so amended, it would read:

> A well regulated Militia, being necessary to the security of a free State, the right of the people to keep and bear Arms *when serving in the Militia* shall not be infringed.

Emotional claims that the right to possess deadly weapons is so important that it is protected by the federal Constitution distort intelligent debate about the wisdom of particular aspects of proposed legislation designed to minimize the slaughter caused by the prevalence of guns in private hands. Those emotional arguments would be nullified by the adoption of my proposed amendment. The amendment certainly would not silence the powerful voice of the gun lobby; it would merely eliminate its ability to advance one mistaken argument.

It is true, of course, that the public's reaction to massacres of schoolchildren, such as the Newtown killings, and the 2013 murder of government employees in the Navy Yard in Washington, D.C., may also introduce a strong emotional element into the debate. That aspect of the debate is, however, based entirely on facts rather than fiction. The law should encourage intelligent discussion of possible remedies for what every American can recognize as an ongoing national tragedy.

The Sandy Hook Elementary School in Newtown, Connecticut, where Adam Lanza killed 26 people, including 20 first-grade students, on December 14, 2012. That incident provided the catalyst for my writing this book. Although the amendment I propose regarding the anti-commandeering principle (see Chapter I) would not have stopped that massacre, it could help prevent others like it, such as the Virginia Tech mass murder in 2007. *(Elizabeth Hallabeck,* Newtown Bee*)*

Appendix

CONSTITUTION OF
THE UNITED STATES[1]

WE THE PEOPLE of the United States, in Order to form a more perfect Union, establish Justice, insure domestic Tranquility, provide for the common defence, promote the general Welfare, and secure the Blessings of Liberty to ourselves and our Posterity, do ordain and establish this Constitution for the United States of America.

ARTICLE I.

SECTION 1. All legislative Powers herein granted shall be vested in a Congress of the United States, which shall consist of a Senate and House of Representatives.

SECTION 2. [1]The House of Representatives

---

1 This text of the Constitution follows the engrossed copy signed by Gen. Washington and the deputies from 12 States. The small superior figures preceding the paragraphs designate clauses, and were not in the original and have no reference to footnotes.

shall be composed of Members chosen every second Year by the People of the several States, and the Electors in each State shall have the Qualifications requisite for Electors of the most numerous Branch of the State Legislature.

[2]No Person shall be a Representative who shall not have attained to the Age of twenty five Years, and been seven Years a Citizen of the United States, and who shall not, when elected, be an Inhabitant of that State in which he shall be chosen.

[3]Representatives and direct Taxes shall be apportioned among the several States which may be included within this Union, according to their respective Numbers, which shall be determined by adding to the whole Number of free Persons, including those bound to Service for a Term of Years, and excluding Indians not taxed, three fifths of all other Persons.[2] The actual Enumeration shall be made within

---

2 The part of this clause relating to the mode of apportionment of representatives among the several States has been affected by section 2 of amendment XIV, and as to taxes on incomes without apportionment by amendment XVI.

three Years after the first Meeting of the Congress of the United States, and within every subsequent Term of ten Years, in such Manner as they shall by Law direct. The Number of Representatives shall not exceed one for every thirty Thousand, but each State shall have at Least one Representative; and until such enumeration shall be made, the State of New Hampshire shall be entitled to chuse three, Massachusetts eight, Rhode Island and Providence Plantations one, Connecticut five, New York six, New Jersey four, Pennsylvania eight, Delaware one, Maryland six, Virginia ten, North Carolina five, South Carolina five, and Georgia three.

[4] When vacancies happen in the Representation from any State, the Executive Authority thereof shall issue Writs of Election to fill such Vacancies.

[5] The House of Representatives shall chuse their Speaker and other Officers; and shall have the sole Power of Impeachment.

SECTION 3. [1] The Senate of the United States shall be composed of two Senators from each

State, chosen by the Legislature thereof[3] for six Years; and each Senator shall have one Vote.

[2] Immediately after they shall be assembled in Consequence of the first Election, they shall be divided as equally as may be into three Classes. The Seats of the Senators of the first Class shall be vacated at the Expiration of the second Year, of the second Class at the Expiration of the fourth Year, and of the third Class at the Expiration of the sixth Year, so that one third may be chosen every second Year; and if Vacancies happen by Resignation or otherwise, during the Recess of the Legislature of any State, the Executive thereof may make temporary Appointments until the next Meeting of the Legislature, which shall then fill such Vacancies.[4]

[3] No Person shall be a Senator who shall not have attained to the Age of thirty Years, and been nine Years a Citizen of the United States,

---

3 This clause has been affected by clause 1 of amendment XVII.

4 This clause has been affected by clause 2 of amendment XVIII.

and who shall not, when elected, be an Inhabitant of that State for which he shall be chosen.

⁴ The Vice President of the United States shall be President of the Senate, but shall have no Vote, unless they be equally divided.

⁵ The Senate shall chuse their other Officers, and also a President pro tempore, in the Absence of the Vice President, or when he shall exercise the Office of President of the United States.

⁶ The Senate shall have the sole Power to try all Impeachments. When sitting for that Purpose, they shall be on Oath or Affirmation. When the President of the United States is tried, the Chief Justice shall preside: And no Person shall be convicted without the Concurrence of two thirds of the Members present.

⁷ Judgment in Cases of Impeachment shall not extend further than to removal from Office, and disqualification to hold and enjoy any Office of honor, Trust or Profit under the United States: but the Party convicted shall nevertheless be liable and subject to Indictment, Trial, Judgment and Punishment, according to Law.

SECTION 4. ¹ The Times, Places and Manner of

holding Elections for Senators and Representatives, shall be prescribed in each State by the Legislature thereof; but the Congress may at any time by Law make or alter such Regulations, except as to the Places of chusing Senators.

[2] The Congress shall assemble at least once in every Year and such Meeting shall be on the first Monday in December,[5] unless they shall by Law appoint a different Day.

SECTION 5. [1] Each House shall be the Judge of the Elections, Returns and Qualifications of its own Members, and a Majority of each shall constitute a Quorum to do Business; but a smaller Number may adjourn from day to day, and may be authorized to compel the Attendance of absent Members, in such Manner, and under such Penalties as each House may provide.

[2] Each House may determine the Rules of its Proceedings, punish its Members for disorderly Behavior, and, with the Concurrence of two thirds, expel a Member.

---

5 This clause has been affected by amendment XX.

³ Each House shall keep a Journal of its Proceedings, and from time to time publish the same, excepting such Parts as may in their Judgment require Secrecy; and the Yeas and Nays of the Members of either House on any question shall, at the Desire of one fifth of those Present, be entered on the Journal.

⁴ Neither House, during the Session of Congress, shall, without the Consent of the other, adjourn for more than three days, nor to any other Place than that in which the two Houses shall be sitting.

SECTION 6. ¹ The Senators and Representatives shall receive a Compensation for their Services, to be ascertained by Law, and paid out of the Treasury of the United States.[6] They shall in all Cases, except Treason, Felony and Breach of the Peace, be privileged from Arrest during their Attendance at the Session of their respective Houses, and in going to and returning from the same; and for any Speech or

---

6 This clause has been affected by amendment XXVII.

Debate in either House, they shall not be questioned in any other Place.

[2] No Senator or Representative shall, during the Time for which he was elected, be appointed to any civil Office under the Authority of the United States, which shall have been created, or the Emoluments whereof shall have been encreased during such time; and no Person holding any Office under the United States, shall be a Member of either House during his Continuance in Office.

SECTION 7. [1]All Bills for raising Revenue shall originate in the House of Representatives; but the Senate may propose or concur with Amendments as on other Bills.

[2] Every Bill which shall have passed the House of Representatives and the Senate, shall, before it become a Law, be presented to the President of the United States; If he approve he shall sign it, but if not he shall return it, with his Objections to that House in which it shall have originated, who shall enter the Objections at large on their Journal, and proceed to reconsider it. If after such Reconsideration two thirds of

that House shall agree to pass the Bill, it shall be sent, together with the Objections, to the other House, by which it shall likewise be reconsidered, and if approved by two thirds of that House, it shall become a Law. But in all such Cases the Votes of both Houses shall be determined by Yeas and Nays, and the Names of the Persons voting for and against the Bill shall be entered on the Journal of each House respectively. If any Bill shall not be returned by the President within ten Days (Sundays excepted) after it shall have been presented to him, the Same shall be a Law, in like Manner as if he had signed it, unless the Congress by their Adjournment prevent its Return, in which Case it shall not be a Law.

[3] Every Order, Resolution, or Vote to which the Concurrence of the Senate and House of Representatives may be necessary (except on a question of Adjournment) shall be presented to the President of the United States; and before the Same shall take Effect, shall be approved by him, or being disapproved by him, shall be repassed by two thirds of the Senate and House

of Representatives, according to the Rules and Limitations prescribed in the Case of a Bill.

SECTION 8. [1] The Congress shall have Power To lay and collect Taxes, Duties, Imposts and Excises, to pay the Debts and provide for the common Defence and general Welfare of the United States; but all Duties, Imposts and Excises shall be uniform throughout the United States;

[2] To borrow Money on the credit of the United States;

[3] To regulate Commerce with foreign Nations, and among the several States, and with the Indian Tribes;

[4] To establish a uniform Rule of Naturalization, and uniform Laws on the subject of Bankruptcies throughout the United States;

[5] To coin Money, regulate the Value thereof, and of foreign Coin, and fix the Standard of Weights and Measures;

[6] To provide for the Punishment of counterfeiting the Securities and current Coin of the United States;

[7] To establish Post Offices and post Roads;

[8] To promote the Progress of Science and useful Arts, by securing for limited Times to Authors and Inventors the exclusive Right to their respective Writings and Discoveries;

[9] To constitute Tribunals inferior to the supreme Court;

[10] To define and punish Piracies and Felonies committed on the high Seas, and Offences against the Law of Nations;

[11] To declare War, grant Letters of Marque and Reprisal, and make Rules concerning Captures on Land and Water;

[12] To raise and support Armies, but no Appropriation of Money to that Use shall be for a longer Term than two Years;

[13] To provide and maintain a Navy;

[14] To make Rules for the Government and Regulation of the land and naval Forces;

[15] To provide for calling forth the Militia to execute the Laws of the Union, suppress Insurrections and repel Invasions;

[16] To provide for organizing, arming, and disciplining, the Militia, and for governing such Part of them as may be employed in the Service

of the United States, reserving to the States respectively, the Appointment of the Officers, and the Authority of training the Militia according to the discipline prescribed by Congress;

[17] To exercise exclusive Legislation in all Cases whatsoever, over such District (not exceeding ten Miles square) as may, by Cession of particular States, and the Acceptance of Congress, become the Seat of the Government of the United States, and to exercise like Authority over all Places purchased by the Consent of the Legislature of the State in which the Same shall be, for the Erection of Forts, Magazines, Arsenals, dock-Yards, and other needful buildings;—And

[18] To make all Laws which shall be necessary and proper for carrying into Execution the foregoing Powers, and all other Powers vested by this Constitution in the Government of the United States, or in any Department or Officer thereof.

SECTION 9. [1] The Migration or Importation of such Persons as any of the States now existing shall think proper to admit, shall not be prohibited by the Congress prior to the Year one thousand eight hundred and eight, but a Tax or duty may be imposed on such Importation, not exceeding ten dollars for each Person.

[2] The Privilege of the Writ of Habeas Corpus shall not be suspended, unless when in Cases of Rebellion or Invasion the public Safety may require it.

[3] No Bill of Attainder or ex post facto Law shall be passed.

[4] No Capitation, or other direct, Tax shall be laid, unless in Proportion to the Census or Enumeration herein before directed to be taken.[7]

[5] No Tax or Duty shall be laid on Articles exported from any State.

[6] No Preference shall be given by any Regulation of Commerce or Revenue to the Ports of one State over those of another: nor shall Vessels bound to, or from, one State, be obliged to enter, clear, or pay Duties in another.

[7] No Money shall be drawn from the Treasury, but in Consequence of Appropriations made by Law; and a regular Statement and

---

7 This clause has been affected by amendment XVI.

Account of the Receipts and Expenditures of all public Money shall be published from time to time.

[8] No Title of Nobility shall be granted by the United States: And no Person holding any Office of Profit or Trust under them, shall, without the Consent of the Congress, accept of any present, Emolument, Office, or Title, of any kind whatever, from any King, Prince, or foreign State.

SECTION 10. [1] No State shall enter into any Treaty, Alliance, or Confederation; grant Letters of Marque and Reprisal; coin Money; emit Bills of Credit; make any Thing but gold and silver Coin a Tender in Payment of Debts; pass any Bill of Attainder, ex post facto Law, or Law impairing the Obligation of Contracts, or grant any Title of Nobility.

[2] No State shall, without the Consent of the Congress, lay any Imposts or Duties on Imports or Exports, except what may be absolutely necessary for executing its inspection Laws: and the net Produce of all Duties and Imposts, laid by any State on Imports or Exports, shall be for the

Use of the Treasury of the United States; and all such Laws shall be subject to the Revision and Control of the Congress.

[3] No State shall, without the Consent of Congress, lay any Duty of Tonnage, keep Troops, or Ships of War in time of Peace, enter into any Agreement or Compact with another State, or with a foreign Power, or engage in War, unless actually invaded, or in such imminent Danger as will not admit of delay.

ARTICLE II.

SECTION 1. [1] The executive Power shall be vested in a President of the United States of America. He shall hold his Office during the Term of four Years, and, together with the Vice President, chosen for the same Term, be elected, as follows

[2] Each State shall appoint, in such Manner as the Legislature thereof may direct, a Number of Electors, equal to the whole Number of Senators and Representatives to which the State may be entitled in the Congress: but no Senator or

Representative, or Person holding an Office of Trust or Profit under the United States, shall be appointed an Elector.

[3] The Electors shall meet in their respective States, and vote by Ballot for two Persons, of whom one at least shall not be an Inhabitant of the same State with themselves. And they shall make a List of all the Persons voted for, and of the Number of Votes for each; which List they shall sign and certify, and transmit sealed to the Seat of the Government of the United States, directed to the President of the Senate. The President of the Senate shall, in the Presence of the Senate and House of Representatives, open all the Certificates, and the Votes shall then be counted. The Person having the greatest Number of Votes shall be the President, if such Number be a Majority of the whole Number of Electors appointed; and if there be more than one who have such Majority, and have an equal Number of Votes, then the House of Representatives shall immediately chuse by Ballot one of them for President; and if no Person have a Majority, then from the five highest on the List

the said House shall in like Manner chuse the President. But in chusing the President, the Votes shall be taken by States, the Representation from each State having one Vote; A quorum for this Purpose shall consist of a Member or Members from two thirds of the States, and a Majority of all the States shall be necessary to a Choice. In every Case, after the Choice of the President, the Person having the greatest Number of Votes of the Electors shall be the Vice President. But if there should remain two or more who have equal Votes, the Senate shall chuse from them by Ballot the Vice President.[8]

[4] The Congress may determine the Time of chusing the Electors, and the Day on which they shall give their Votes; which Day shall be the same throughout the United States.

[5] No Person except a natural born Citizen, or a Citizen of the United States, at the time of the Adoption of this Constitution, shall be eligible to the Office of President; neither shall any Person be eligible to that Office who shall not have

---

8 This clause has been superseded by amendment XII.

attained to the Age of thirty five Years, and been fourteen Years a Resident within the United States.

[6] In Case of the Removal of the President from Office, or of his Death, Resignation, or Inability to discharge the Powers and Duties of the said Office,[9] the Same shall devolve on the Vice President, and the Congress may by Law provide for the Case of Removal, Death, Resignation or Inability, both of the President and Vice President, declaring what Officer shall then act as President, and such Officer shall act accordingly, until the Disability be removed, or a President shall be elected.

[7] The President shall, at stated Times, receive for his Services, a Compensation, which shall neither be encreased nor diminished during the Period for which he shall have been elected, and he shall not receive within that Period any other Emolument from the United States, or any of them.

[8] Before he enter on the Execution of his

---

9 This clause has been affected by amendment XXV.

Office, he shall take the following Oath or Affirmation: — "I do solemnly swear (or affirm) that I will faithfully execute the Office of President of the United States, and will to the best of my Ability, preserve, protect and defend the Constitution of the United States."

SECTION 2. [1] The President shall be Commander in Chief of the Army and Navy of the United States, and of the Militia of the several States, when called into the actual Service of the United States; he may require the Opinion, in writing, of the principal Officer in each of the executive Departments, upon any Subject relating to the Duties of their respective Offices, and he shall have Power to grant Reprieves and Pardons for Offences against the United States, except in Cases of Impeachment.

[2] He shall have Power, by and with the Advice and Consent of the Senate, to make Treaties, provided two thirds of the Senators present concur; and he shall nominate, and by and with the Advice and Consent of the Senate, shall appoint Ambassadors, other public Ministers and Consuls, Judges of the supreme Court, and all other

Officers of the United States, whose Appointments are not herein otherwise provided for, and which shall be established by Law: but the Congress may by Law vest the Appointment of such inferior Officers, as they think proper, in the President alone, in the Courts of Law, or in the Heads of Departments.

[3] The President shall have Power to fill up all Vacancies that may happen during the Recess of the Senate, by granting Commissions which shall expire at the End of their next Session.

SECTION 3. He shall from time to time give to the Congress Information of the State of the Union, and recommend to their Consideration such Measures as he shall judge necessary and expedient; he may, on extraordinary Occasions, convene both Houses, or either of them, and in Case of Disagreement between them, with Respect to the Time of Adjournment, he may adjourn them to such Time as he shall think proper; he shall receive Ambassadors and other public Ministers; he shall take Care that the Laws be faithfully executed, and shall Commission all the Officers of the United States.

SECTION 4. The President, Vice President and all civil Officers of the United States, shall be removed from Office on Impeachment for, and Conviction of, Treason, Bribery, or other high Crimes and Misdemeanors.

ARTICLE III.

SECTION 1. The judicial Power of the United States, shall be vested in one supreme Court, and in such inferior Courts as the Congress may from time to time ordain and establish. The Judges, both of the supreme and inferior Courts, shall hold their Offices during good Behaviour, and shall, at stated Times, receive for their Services, a Compensation, which shall not be diminished during their Continuance in Office.

SECTION 2. [1] The judicial Power shall extend to all Cases, in Law and Equity, arising under this Constitution, the Laws of the United States, and Treaties made, or which shall be made, under their Authority;— to all Cases affecting Ambassadors, other public Ministers and Con- suls;— to all Cases of admiralty and maritime

Jurisdiction;—to Controversies to which the United States will be a party;—to Controversies between two or more States;—between a State and Citizens of another State;[10]—between Citizens of different States,—between Citizens of the same State claiming Lands under Grants of different States, and between a State, or the Citizens thereof, and foreign States, Citizens or Subjects.

[2] In all Cases affecting Ambassadors, other public Ministers and Consuls, and those in which a State shall be Party, the supreme Court shall have original Jurisdiction. In all the other Cases before mentioned, the supreme Court shall have appellate Jurisdiction, both as to Law and Fact, with such Exceptions, and under such Regulations as the Congress shall make.

[3] The Trial of all Crimes, except in Cases of Impeachment, shall be by Jury; and such Trial shall be held in the State where the said Crimes shall have been committed; but when not committed within any State, the Trial shall be at

---

10 This clause has been affected by amendment XI.

such Place or Places as the Congress may by Law have directed.

SECTION 3. [1] Treason against the United States, shall consist only in levying War against them, or in adhering to their Enemies, giving them Aid and Comfort. No Person shall be convicted of Treason unless on the Testimony of two Witnesses to the same overt Act, or on Confession in open Court.

[2] The Congress shall have Power to declare the Punishment of Treason, but no Attainder of Treason shall work Corruption of Blood, or Forfeiture except during the Life of the Person attainted.

ARTICLE IV.

SECTION 1. Full Faith and Credit shall be given in each State to the public Acts, Records, and judicial Proceedings of every other State. And the Congress may by general Laws prescribe the Manner in which such Acts, Records and Proceedings shall be proved, and the Effect thereof.

SECTION 2. [1] The Citizens of each State shall be entitled to all Privileges and Immunities of Citizens in the several States.

[2] A Person charged in any State with Treason, Felony, or other Crime, who shall flee from Justice, and be found in another State, shall on Demand of the executive Authority of the State from which he fled, be delivered up, to be removed to the State having Jurisdiction of the Crime.

[3] No Person held to Service or Labour in one State, under the Laws thereof, escaping into another, shall, in Consequence of any Law, or Regulation therein, be discharged from such Service or Labour, but shall be delivered up on Claim of the Party to whom such Service or Labour may be due.[11]

SECTION 3. [1] New States may be admitted by the Congress into this Union; but no new State shall be formed or erected within the Jurisdiction of any other State; nor any State be formed by the Junction of two or more States, or Parts of States, without the Consent of the

---

11 This clause has been affected by amendment XIII.

Legislatures of the States concerned as well as of the Congress.

² The Congress shall have Power to dispose of and make all needful Rules and Regulations respecting the Territory or other Property belonging to the United States; and nothing in this Constitution shall be so construed as to Prejudice any Claims of the United States, or of any particular State.

SECTION 4. The United States shall guarantee to every State in this Union a Republican Form of Government, and shall protect each of them against Invasion; and on Application of the Legislature, or of the Executive (when the Legislature cannot be convened) against domestic Violence.

ARTICLE V.

The Congress, whenever two thirds of both Houses shall deem it necessary, shall propose Amendments to this Constitution, or, on the Application of the Legislatures of two thirds of the several States, shall call a Convention for proposing Amendments, which, in either Case, shall be valid to all Intents and Purposes, as Part of this Constitution, when ratified by the Legislatures of three fourths of the several States, or by Conventions in three fourths thereof, as the one or the other Mode of Ratification may be proposed by the Congress; Provided that no Amendment which may be made prior to the Year One thousand eight hundred and eight shall in any Manner affect the first and fourth Clauses in the Ninth Section of the first Article; and that no State, without its Consent, shall be deprived of its equal Suffrage in the Senate.

ARTICLE VI.

[1]All Debts contracted and Engagements entered into, before the Adoption of this Constitution, shall be as valid against the United States under this Constitution, as under the Confederation.

[2] This Constitution, and the Laws of the United States which shall be made in Pursuance thereof; and all Treaties made, or which shall be

made, under the Authority of the United States, shall be the supreme Law of the Land; and the Judges in every State shall be bound thereby, any Thing in the Constitution or Laws of any State to the Contrary notwithstanding.

[3] The Senators and Representatives before mentioned, and the Members of the several State Legislatures, and all executive and judicial Officers, both of the United States and of the several States, shall be bound by Oath or Affirmation, to support this Constitution; but no religious Test shall ever be required as a Qualification to any Office or public Trust under the United States.

ARTICLE VII.

The Ratification of the Conventions of nine States, shall be sufficient for the Establishment of this Constitution between the States so ratifying the Same.

DONE in Convention by the Unanimous Consent of the States present the Seventeenth

Day of September in the Year of our Lord one thousand seven hundred and Eighty seven and of the Independence of the United States of America the Twelfth

IN WITNESS whereof We have hereunto subscribed our Names,

G^O. WASHINGTON — Presid^t.
and deputy from Virginia

[Signed also by the deputies of
twelve States.]

Delaware

Geo: Read, Gunning Bedford Jun, John
Dickinson, Richard Bassett, Jaco: Broom

Maryland

James McHenry, Dan of St Thos Jenifer,
Danl Carroll

Virginia

John Blair, James Madison Jr.

North Carolina

Wm Blount, Rich^d. Dobbs Spaight, Hu
Williamson

South Carolina

J. Rutledge, Charles Cotesworth Pinckney,
Charles
Pinckney, Pierce Butler

Georgia

William Few, Abr Baldwin

New Hampshire
John Langdon, Nicholas Gilman

Massachusetts
Nathaniel Gorham, Rufus King

Connecticut
W^m. Saml. Johnson, Roger Sherman

New York
Alexander Hamilton

New Jersey
Wil: Livingston, David Brearley, W^m. Paterson, Jona: Dayton

Pennsylvania
B Franklin, Thomas Mifflin, Robt Morris, Geo. Clymer, Thos. Fitzsimons, Jared Ingersoll, James Wilson, Gouv Morris

Attest: William Jackson *Secretary*

Articles in addition to, and Amendment of, the Constitution of the United States of America, proposed by Congress, and ratified by the Legislatures of the several states, pursuant to the fifth Article of the original Constitution

ARTICLE [I.][12]

Congress shall make no law respecting an establishment of religion, or prohibiting the free exercise thereof; or abridging the freedom of speech, or of the press; of the right of the people peaceably to assemble, and to petition the Government for a redress of grievances.

ARTICLE [II.]

A well regulated Militia, being necessary to the security of a free State, the right of the people to keep and bear Arms, shall not be infringed.

---

12 Only the 13th, 14th, 15th, and 16th articles of amendment had numbers assigned to them at the time of ratification.

ARTICLE [III.]

No Soldier shall, in time of peace be quartered in any house, without the consent of the Owner, nor in time of war, but in a manner to be prescribed by law.

ARTICLE [IV.]

The right of the people to be secure in their persons, houses, papers, and effects, against unreasonable searches and seizures, shall not be violated, and no Warrants shall issue, but upon probable cause, supported by Oath or affirmation, and particularly describing the place to be searched, and the persons or things to be seized.

ARTICLE [V.]

No person shall be held to answer for a capital, or otherwise infamous crime, unless on a presentment or indictment of a Grand Jury, except in cases arising in the land or naval forces, or in the Militia, when in actual service in time of War or public danger; nor shall any person be subject for the same offence to be twice put in jeopardy of life or limb; nor shall be compelled in any criminal case to be a witness against himself, nor be deprived of life, liberty, or property, without due process of law; nor shall private property be taken for public use, without just compensation.

ARTICLE [VI.]

In all criminal prosecutions, the accused shall enjoy the right to a speedy and public trial, by an impartial jury of the State and district wherein the crime shall have been committed, which district shall have been previously ascertained by law, and to be informed of the nature and cause of the accusation; to be confronted with the witnesses against him; to have compulsory process for obtaining witnesses in his favor, and to have the Assistance of Counsel for his defense.

ARTICLE [VII.]

In Suits at common law, where the value in controversy shall exceed twenty dollars, the right of trial by jury shall be preserved, and no fact tried by a jury, shall be otherwise re-examined in any Court of the United States, than according to the rules of the common law.

ARTICLE [VIII.]

Excessive bail shall not be required, nor excessive fines imposed, nor cruel and unusual punishments inflicted.

ARTICLE [IX.]

The enumeration in the Constitution, of certain rights, shall not be construed to deny or disparage others retained by the people.

ARTICLE [X.]

The powers not delegated to the United States by the Constitution, nor prohibited by it to the States, are reserved to the States respectively, or to the people.

ARTICLE [XI.]

The Judicial power of the United States shall not be construed to extend to any suit in law or equity, commenced or prosecuted against one of the United States by Citizens of another State, or by Citizens or Subjects of any Foreign State.

ARTICLE [XII.]

The Electors shall meet in their respective states, and vote by ballot for President and Vice-President, one of whom, at least, shall not be an inhabitant of the same state with themselves; they shall name in their ballots the person voted for as President, and in distinct ballots the person voted for as Vice-President, and they shall make distinct lists of all persons voted for as President, and of all persons voted for as Vice-President, and of the number of votes for each, which lists they shall sign and certify, and transmit sealed to the seat of the government of the United States, directed to the President of the Senate;—The President of the Senate shall, in the presence of the Senate and House of Representatives, open all the certificates and the votes shall then be counted;—The person having the greatest number of votes for President, shall be the President, if such number be a majority of the whole number of Electors appointed; and if no person have such majority, then from the persons having the highest numbers not exceeding three on the list of those voted for as President, the House of Representatives shall choose immediately, by ballot, the President. But in choosing the President, the votes shall be taken by states, the representation from each state having one vote; a quorum for this purpose shall consist of a member or members from two-thirds of the states, and a majority of all the states shall be necessary to a choice. And if the House of Representatives shall not choose a President whenever the right of choice shall devolve upon them, before the fourth day of March next following, then the Vice-President shall act as President, as in the case of the death or other constitutional disability of the President.[13] — The person having the greatest number of votes as Vice-President, shall be the Vice-President, if such

---

13 This sentence has been superseded by section 3 of amendment XX.

number be a majority of the whole number of Electors appointed, and if no person have a majority, then from the two highest numbers on the list, the Senate shall choose the Vice-President; a quorum for the purpose shall consist of two-thirds of the whole number of Senators, and a majority of the whole number shall be necessary to a choice. But no person constitutionally ineligible to the office of President shall be eligible to that of Vice-President of the United States.

ARTICLE XIII.

SECTION 1. Neither slavery nor involuntary servitude, except as a punishment for crime whereof the party shall have been duly convicted, shall exist within the United States, or any place subject to their jurisdiction.

SECTION 2. Congress shall have power to enforce this article by appropriate legislation.

ARTICLE XIV.

SECTION 1. All persons born or naturalized in the United States, and subject to the jurisdiction thereof, are citizens of the United States and of the State wherein they reside. No State shall make or enforce any law which shall abridge the privileges or immunities of citizens of the United States; nor shall any State deprive any person of life, liberty, or property, without due process of law; nor deny to any person within its jurisdiction the equal protection of the laws.

SECTION 2. Representatives shall be apportioned among the several States according to their respective numbers, counting the whole number of persons in each State, excluding Indians not taxed. But when the right to vote at any election for the choice of electors for President and Vice President of the United States, Representatives in Congress, the Executive and Judicial officers of a State, or the members of the Legislature thereof, is denied to any of the male inhabitants of such State, being twenty-one years of age,[14] and citizens of the United States, or in any way abridged, except for participation

---

14 See amendment XIX and section 1 of amendment XXVI.

in rebellion, or other crime, the basis of representation therein shall be reduced in the proportion which the number of such male citizens shall bear to the whole number of male citizens twenty-one years of age in such State.

SECTION 3. No person shall be a Senator or Representative in Congress, or elector of President and Vice President, or hold any office, civil or military, under the United States, or under any State, who, having previously taken an oath, as a member of Congress, or as an officer of the United States, or as a member of any State legislature, or as an executive or judicial officer of any State, to support the Constitution of the United States, shall have engaged in insurrection or rebellion against the same, or given aid or comfort to the enemies thereof. But Congress may by a vote of two-thirds of each House, remove such disability.

SECTION 4. The validity of the public debt of the United States, authorized by law, including debts incurred for payment of pensions and bounties for services in suppressing insurrection or rebellion, shall not be questioned. But neither the United States nor any State shall assume or pay any debt or obligation incurred in aid of insurrection or rebellion against the United States, or any claim for the loss or emancipation of any slave; but all such debts, obligations and claims shall be held illegal and void.

SECTION 5. The Congress shall have power to enforce, by appropriate legislation, the provisions of this article.

ARTICLE XV.

SECTION 1. The right of citizens of the United States to vote shall not be denied or abridged by the United States or by any State on account of race, color, or previous condition of servitude.

SECTION 2. The Congress shall have power to enforce this article by appropriate legislation.

ARTICLE XVI.

The Congress shall have power to lay and collect taxes on incomes, from whatever source derived, without apportionment among the several States, and without regard to any census or enumeration.

ARTICLE [XVII.]

The Senate of the United States shall be composed of two Senators from each State, elected by the people thereof, for six years; and each Senator shall have one vote. The electors in each State shall have the qualifications requisite for electors of the most numerous branch of the State legislatures.

When vacancies happen in the representation of any State in the Senate, the executive authority of such State shall issue writs of election to fill such vacancies: Provided, That the legislature of any State may empower the executive thereof to make temporary appointments until the people fill the vacancies by election as the legislature may direct.

This amendment shall not be so construed as to affect the election or term of any Senator chosen before it becomes valid as part of the Constitution.

ARTICLE [XVIII.][15]

SECTION 1. After one year from the ratification of this article the manufacture, sale, or transportation of intoxicating liquors within, the importation thereof into, or the exportation thereof from the United States and all territory subject to the jurisdiction thereof for beverage purposes is hereby prohibited.

SECTION 2. The Congress and the several States shall have concurrent power to enforce this article by appropriate legislation.

SECTION 3. This article shall be inoperative unless it shall have been ratified as an amendment to the Constitution by the legislatures of the several States, as provided in the Constitution, within seven years from the date of the submission hereof to the States by the Congress.

ARTICLE [XIX.]

The right of citizens of the United States to

---

15 Repealed by section 1 of amendment XXI.

vote shall not be denied or abridged by the United States or by any State on account of sex.

Congress shall have power to enforce this article by appropriate legislation.

ARTICLE [XX.]

SECTION 1. The terms of the President and Vice President shall end at noon on the 20th day of January, and the terms of Senators and Representatives at noon on the 3d day of January, of the years in which such terms would have ended if this article had not been ratified; and the terms of their successors shall then begin.

SECTION 2. The Congress shall assemble at least once in every year, and such meeting shall begin at noon on the 3d day of January, unless they shall by law appoint a different day.

SECTION 3. If, at the time fixed for the beginning of the term of the President, the President elect shall have died, the Vice President elect shall become President. If a President shall not have been chosen before the time fixed for the beginning of his term, or if the President elect shall have failed to qualify, then the Vice President elect shall act as President until a President shall have qualified; and the Congress may by law provide for the case wherein neither a President elect nor a Vice President elect shall have qualified, declaring who shall then act as President, or the manner in which one who is to act shall be selected, and such person shall act accordingly until a President or Vice President shall have qualified.

SECTION 4. The Congress may by law provide for the case of the death of any of the persons from whom the House of Representatives may choose a President whenever the right of choice shall have devolved upon them, and for the case of the death of any of the persons from whom the Senate may choose a Vice President whenever the right of choice shall have devolved upon them.

SECTION 5. Sections 1 and 2 shall take effect on the 15th day of October following the ratification of this article.

SECTION 6. This article shall be inoperative unless it shall have been ratified as an amendment to the Constitution by the legislatures of three-fourths of the several States within seven years from the date of its submission.

ARTICLE [XXI.]

SECTION 1. The eighteenth article of amendment to the Constitution of the United States is hereby repealed.

SECTION 2. The transportation or importation into any State, Territory, or possession of the United States for delivery or use therein of intoxicating liquors, in violation of the laws thereof, is hereby prohibited.

SECTION 3. This article shall be inoperative unless it shall have been ratified as an amendment to the Constitution by conventions in the several States, as provided in the Constitution, within seven years from the date of the submission hereof to the States by the Congress.

ARTICLE [XXII.]

SECTION 1. No person shall be elected to the office of the President more than twice, and no person who has held the office of President, or acted as President, for more than two years of a term of which some other person was elected President shall be elected to the office of the President more than once. But this Article shall not apply to any person holding the office of President when this Article was proposed by the Congress, and shall not prevent any person who may be holding the office of President, or acting as President, during the term within which this Article becomes operative from holding the office of President or acting as President during the remainder of such term.

SECTION 2. This article shall be inoperative unless it shall have been ratified as an amendment to the Constitution by the legislatures of three-fourths of the several States within seven years from the date of its submission to the States by the Congress.

ARTICLE [XXIII.]

SECTION 1. The District constituting the seat of Government of the United States shall appoint in such manner as the Congress may direct:

A number of electors of President and Vice President equal to the whole number of Senators and Representatives in Congress to which the District would be entitled if it were a State, but in no event more than the least populous State; they shall be in addition to those appointed by the States, but they shall be considered, for the purposes of the election of President and Vice President, to be electors appointed by a State; and they shall meet in the District and perform such duties as provided by the twelfth article of amendment.

SECTION 2. The Congress shall have power to enforce this article by appropriate legislation.

ARTICLE [XXIV.]

SECTION 1. The right of citizens of the United States to vote in any primary or other election for President or Vice President, for electors for President or Vice President, or for Senator or Representative in Congress, shall not be denied or abridged by the United States or any State by reason of failure to pay any poll tax or other tax.

SECTION 2. The Congress shall have power to enforce this article by appropriate legislation.

ARTICLE [XXV.]

SECTION 1. In case of the removal of the President from office or of his death or resignation, the Vice President shall become President.

SECTION 2. Whenever there is a vacancy in the office of the Vice President, the President shall nominate a Vice President who shall take office upon confirmation by a majority vote of both Houses of Congress.

SECTION 3. Whenever the President transmits to the President pro tempore of the Senate and the Speaker of the House of Representatives his written declaration that he is unable to discharge the powers and duties of his office, and until he transmits to them a written declaration to the contrary, such powers and duties shall be discharged by the Vice President as Acting President.

SECTION 4. Whenever the Vice President and a majority of either the principal officers of the executive departments or of such other body as Congress may by law provide, transmit to the President pro tempore of the Senate and the Speaker of the House of Representatives their written declaration that the President is unable to discharge the powers and duties of his office, the Vice President shall immediately assume the powers and duties of the office as Acting President.

Thereafter, when the President transmits to the President pro tempore of the Senate and the Speaker of the House of Representatives his written declaration that no inability exists, he shall resume the powers and duties of his office unless the Vice President and a majority of either the principal officers of the executive department[16] or of such other body as Congress may by law provide, transmit within four days to the President pro tempore of the Senate and the Speaker of the House of Representatives their written declaration that the President is unable to discharge the powers and duties of his office.

---

16 So in original. Probably should be "departments."

Thereupon Congress shall decide the issue, assembling within forty-eight hours for that purpose if not in session. If the Congress, within twenty-one days after receipt of the latter written declaration, or, if Congress is not in session, within twenty-one days after Congress is required to assemble, determines by two-thirds vote of both Houses that the President is unable to discharge the powers and duties of his office, the Vice President shall continue to discharge the same as Acting President; otherwise, the President shall resume the powers and duties of his office.

ARTICLE [XXVI.]

SECTION 1. The right of citizens of the United States, who are eighteen years of age or older, to vote shall not be denied or abridged by the United States or by any State on account of age.

SECTION 2. The Congress shall have power to enforce this article by appropriate legislation.

ARTICLE [XXVII.]

No law, varying the compensation for the services of the Senators and Representatives, shall take effect, until an election of Representatives shall have intervened.

Acknowledgments

In a postscript to *Five Chiefs* I expressed my gratitude to several people who helped me complete that book—Supreme Court Library assistants Catherine Romano and Sara Sonet; Steve Petteway, the Court photographer; John Boulanger, who kept my computer working; my agent Peter Bernstein; my editor Geoff Shandler; my secretary Janice Harley; my aide to Chambers Peter Edwards; and my beautiful dietitian, who happens to be married to me. All of them have again earned my thanks for helping with this book. I also owe special thanks to Eduardo Bruera, my law clerk during the 2012 term of the Court, and to Aaron Zelinsky, my current clerk. Identifying these participants in the process that produced the explanation of my proposed amendments to the Constitution has reminded me of how much I am indebted to the 122 exceptional lawyers who have played an indispensable role in my work as a judge during my entire career. I have always been especially proud of my ability to pick good law clerks. If you recognize any of the names on the following list, you will understand why.

United States Court of Appeals Law Clerks:

1970 Term: Gary Senner; **1971 Term:** Samuel Clapper; **1972 Term:** James Kitch; **1973 Term:** Stephen Goldman; **1973 and 1974 Terms:** Robert Garrett; **1974 Term:** James Whitehead; **1975 Term:** Sharon Baldwin, Charles "Skip" Paul.

Supreme Court Law Clerks:

1975 Term: Sharon Baldwin, Charles "Skip" Paul, George Rutherglen; **1976 Term:** Daniel

Farber, Gregory Huffaker, Jr., David Kirby; **1977 Term:** Stewart Baker, Francis Blake, John Muench; **1978 Term:** Susan Estrich, James Liebman; **1979 Term:** Peter Isakoff, Michele Odorizzi; **1980 Term:** Jeffrey Tone, Constantine Trela; **1981 Term:** David DeBruin, Matthew Verschelden; **1982 Term:** Carol Lee, Jeffrey Lehman; **1983 Term:** Lawrence Rosenthal, John Schaibley III; **1984 Term:** Richard Kapnick, James McCollum, Jr.; **1985 Term:** Stephen Marzen, Clifford Sloan; **1986 Term:** Ronald Lee, Lawrence Marshall; **1987 Term:** Abner Greene, Teresa Wynn Roseborough; **Jan. 1987 to Jan. 1988:** Randolph Moss; **1988 Term:** Diane Amann; **Jan. 1988 to Jan. 1989:** Lewis Liman; **1989 Term:** Christopher Eisgruber, Marina Hsieh; **1990 Term:** Preeta Bansal, Matthew Roberts; **1990 and 1991 Terms:** Nancy Marder; **1991 Term:** Kathleen Moriarty Mueller, Robert Schapiro, Peter Yu; **1992 Term:** Pamela Harris, Stephen Reily, Douglas Winthrop; **1993 Term:** Sean Donahue, Daniel Klerman, Corinne Beckwith; **1994 Term:** Ian Gershengorn, Gregory Magarian, Craig Singer; **1995 Term:** David

Barron, Jeffrey Dobbins, Eileen Mullen; **1996 Term:** Melissa Hart, Olatunde Johnson, Jonathan Levitsky; **1997 Term:** Elizabeth Cavanagh, David Friedman, Christopher Meade; **1998 Term:** Jeffrey Fisher, Allison Marston Danner, Adam Samaha; **1999 Term:** Deborah Pearlstein, Joshua Waldman, Sonja West; **2000 Term:** Eduardo Penalver, Andrew Siegel, Anne Voigts; **2001 Term:** Kathleen Hartnett, Alison Nathan, Edward Siskel; **2002 Term:** Troy McKenzie, Eric Olson, Kathryn Tongue Watts, Amy Wildermuth; **2003 Term:** Leondra Kruger, Amanda Cohen Leiter, Margaret Lemos, Benjamin Mizer; **2004 Term:** Melissa Arbus Sherry, Roberto Gonzalez, Michael Gottlieb, Daniel Powell; **2005 Term:** Jean Galbraith, Daniel Lenerz, Sarah McCallum, Samuel Spital; **2006 Term:** Nicholas Bagley, Chad Golder, Jamal Greene, Lauren Sudeall Lucas; **2007 Term:** Todd Gluth, Sara Klein Eisenberg, Kate Shaw, Abby Wright; **2008 Term:** Jessica Bulman-Pozen, Cecelia Klingele, Lindsey Powell, Damian Williams; **2009 Term:** Adam Jed, Hyland Hunt, Merritt McAlister, David Pozen; **2010 Term:** Sam

Erman; **2011 Term:** Dina Mishra; **2012 Term:** Eduardo Bruera; and **2013 Term:** Aaron Zelinsky.

I am also indebted to Nellie Pitts, who moved from Chicago to Washington in 1975 to work as my secretary until she retired in 2006, and to the following clerks who were hired by retired Justices Potter Stewart, Lewis Powell, and Byron White, but spent most of their time working for me.

Jan. 1983 to Jan. 1984: Rory Little (Justice Stewart)

1990 Term: George Freeman III (Justice Powell)

1993 Term: Deanne Maynard (Justice Powell)

1994 Term: James Benjamin (Justice Powell)

1995 Term: Mark Harris (Justice Powell)

1996 Term: John Flynn (Justice White)

1997 Term: Benjamin Powell (Justice White)

1998 Term: Cara Robertson (Justice White)

1999 Term: J. Brett Busby (Justice White)

2000 Term: Joseph Thai (Justice White)

About the Author

———◄◦►———

John Paul Stevens served as a judge on the United States Court of Appeals for the Seventh Circuit from 1970 to 1975. President Ford nominated him as an associate justice of the Supreme Court, and he took his seat on December 19, 1975. Justice Stevens retired from the Supreme Court on June 29, 2010. He is the author of a memoir, *Five Chiefs*.

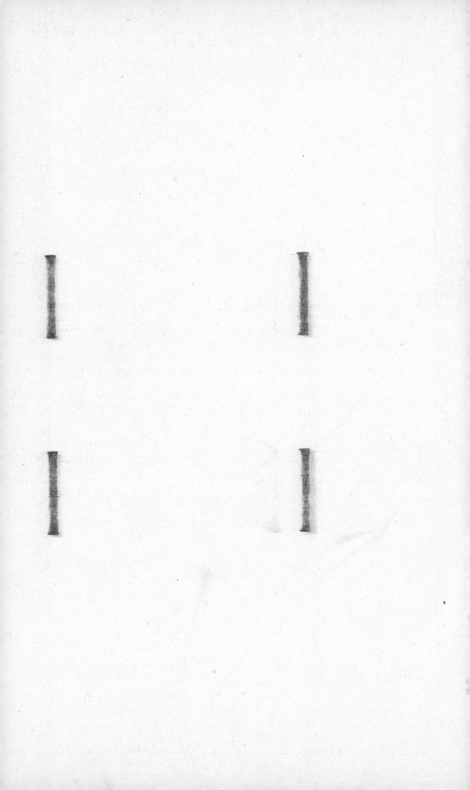